MONEy

Workbook

This Book Belongs To:

TABLE OF CONTENTS

ANSWER KEY IN BACK

Name:............................... $ 🗎 💰 $ **Date:** ....

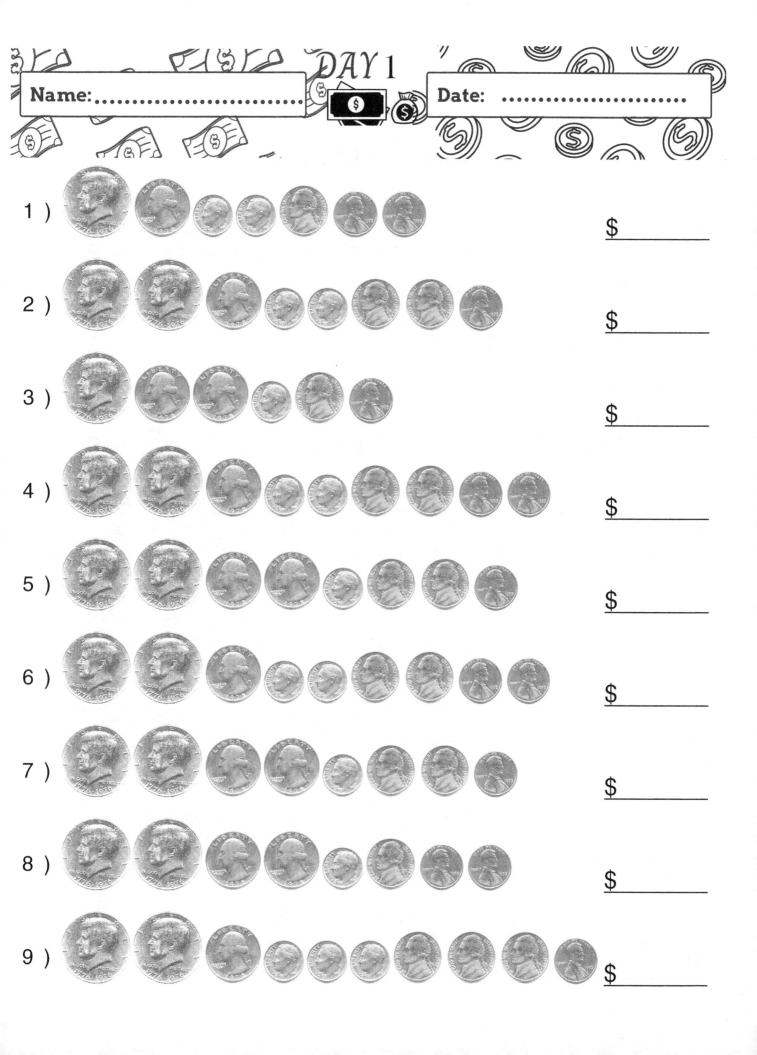

1) $ _____

2) $ _____

3) $ _____

4) $ _____

5) $ _____

6) $ _____

7) $ _____

8) $ _____

9) $ _____

DAY 2

Name: .... $ **Date:** ....

Count the Money

1) 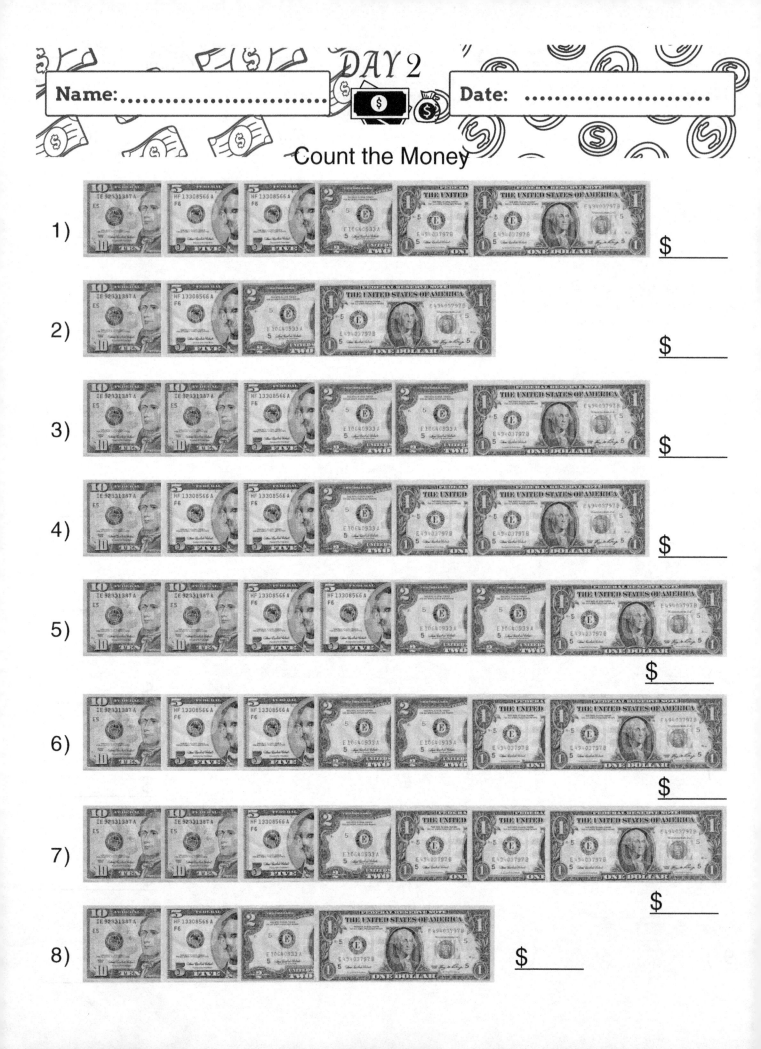 $ _____

2) $ _____

3) $ _____

4) $ _____

5) $ _____

6) $ _____

7) $ _____

8) $ _____

Name:...................................   Date: ....

1) 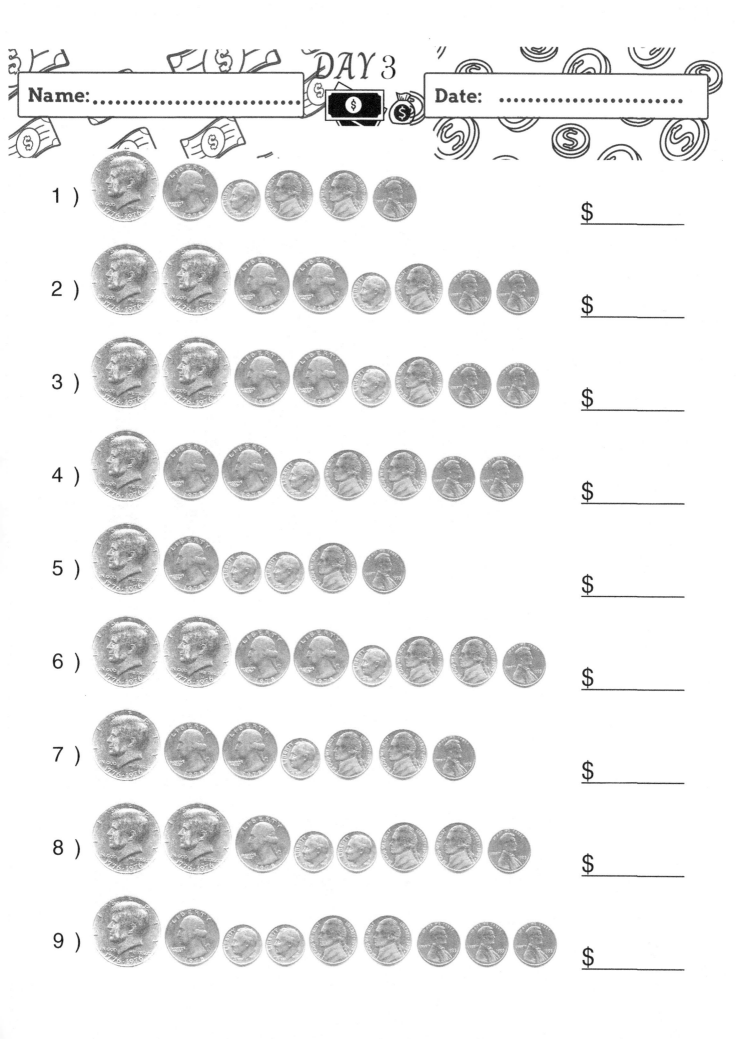 $ _____

2) $ _____

3) $ _____

4) $ _____

5) $ _____

6) $ _____

7) $ _____

8) $ _____

9) $ _____

Name:......................... **Date:** ....

Count the Money

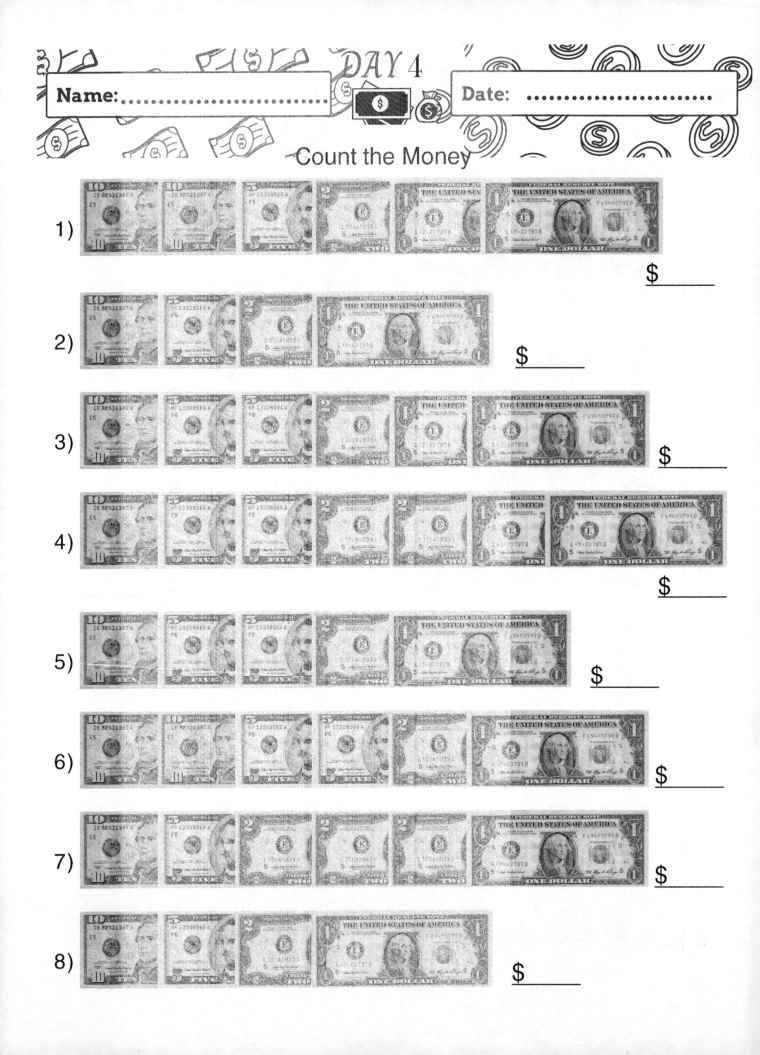

1) $ _____

2) $ _____

3) $ _____

4) $ _____

5) $ _____

6) $ _____

7) $ _____

8) $ _____

Name:................................ **Date:** ....

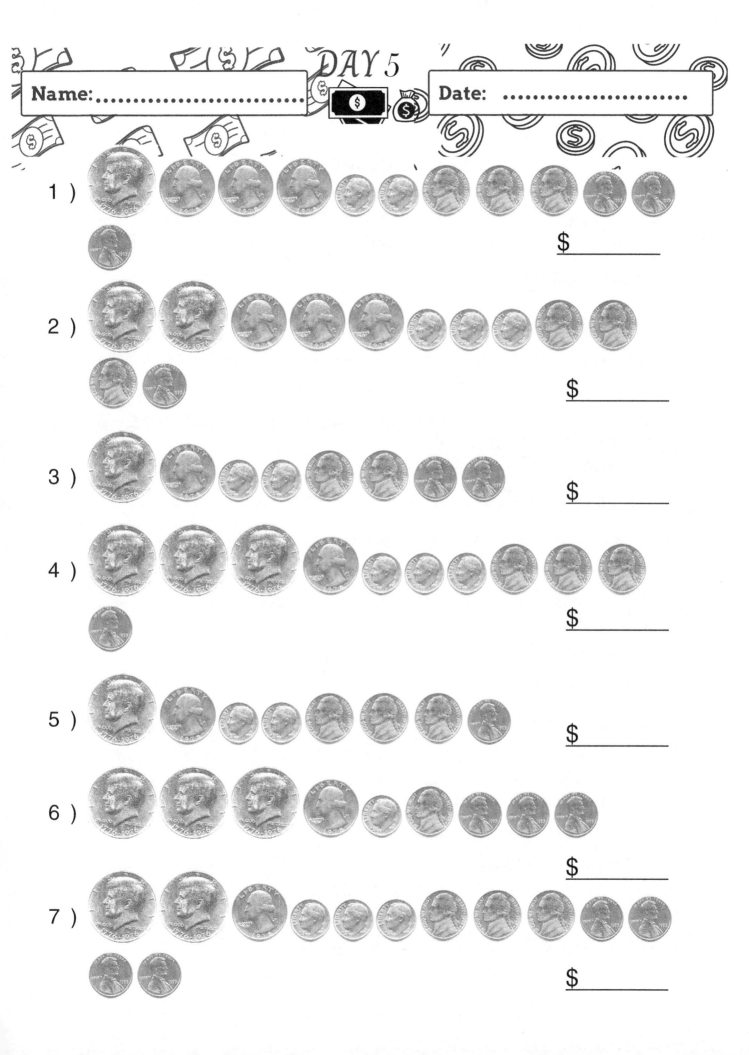

1) $ _____

2) $ _____

3) $ _____

4) $ _____

5) $ _____

6) $ _____

7) $ _____

Name: ....

Date: ....

Count the Money

1) $ _____

2) $ _____

3) $ _____

4) $ _____

5) $ _____

Name:................................

Date: ....

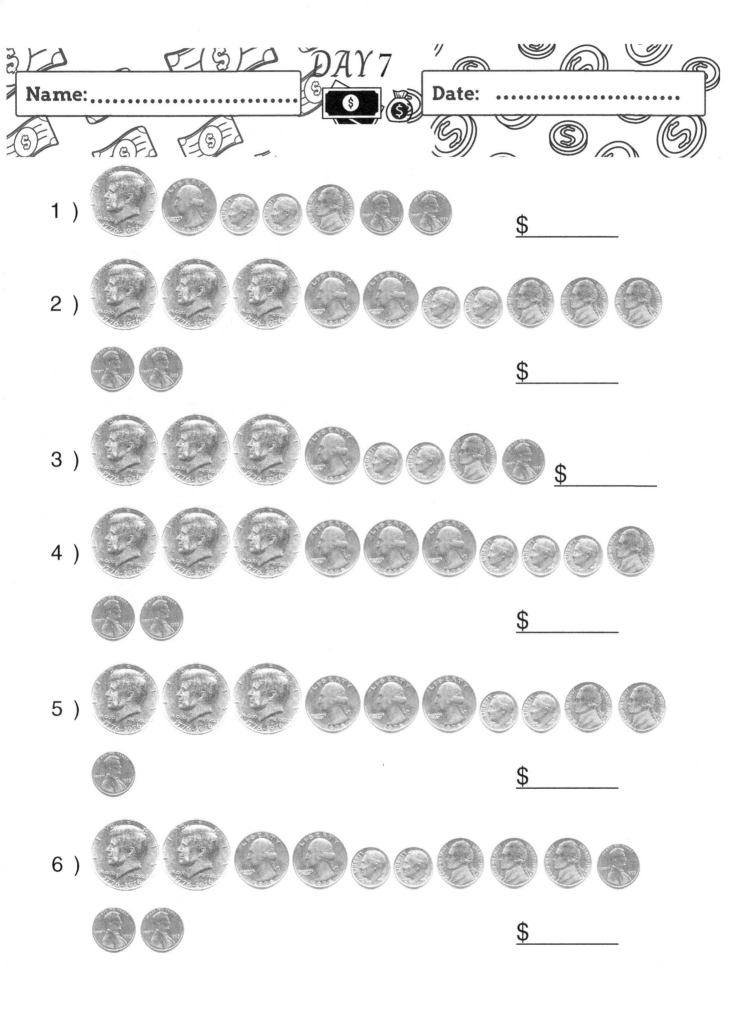

1) $ _____

2) $ _____

3) $ _____

4) $ _____

5) $ _____

6) $ _____

Name: .... **Date:** ....

Count the Money

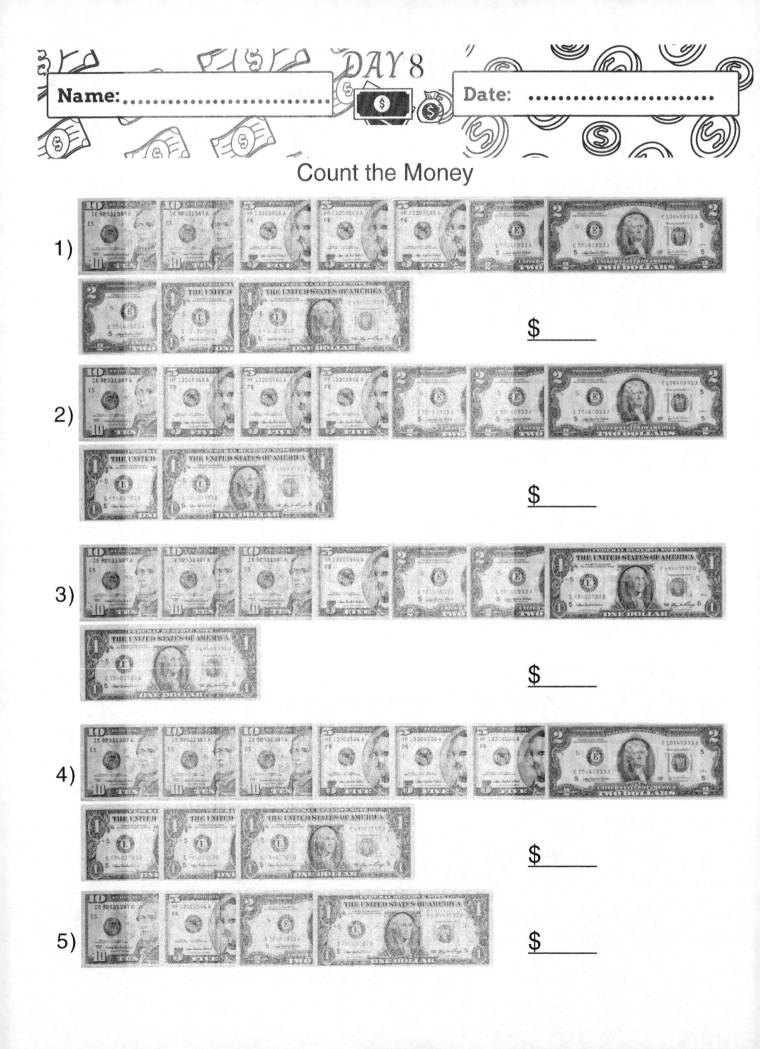

1) $ _____

2) $ _____

3) $ _____

4) $ _____

5) $ _____

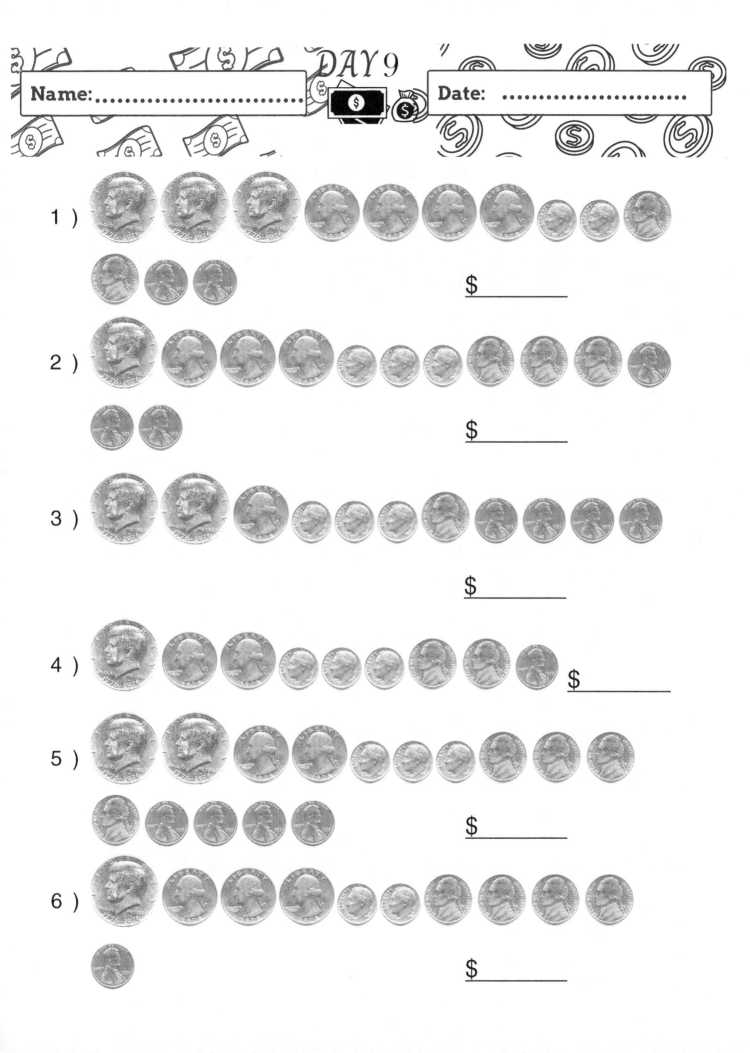

Name:............................

DAY 9

Date: ....

1)

$ _____

2)

$ _____

3)

$ _____

4)

$ _____

5)

$ _____

6)

$ _____

Name: ....

Date: ....

Count the Money

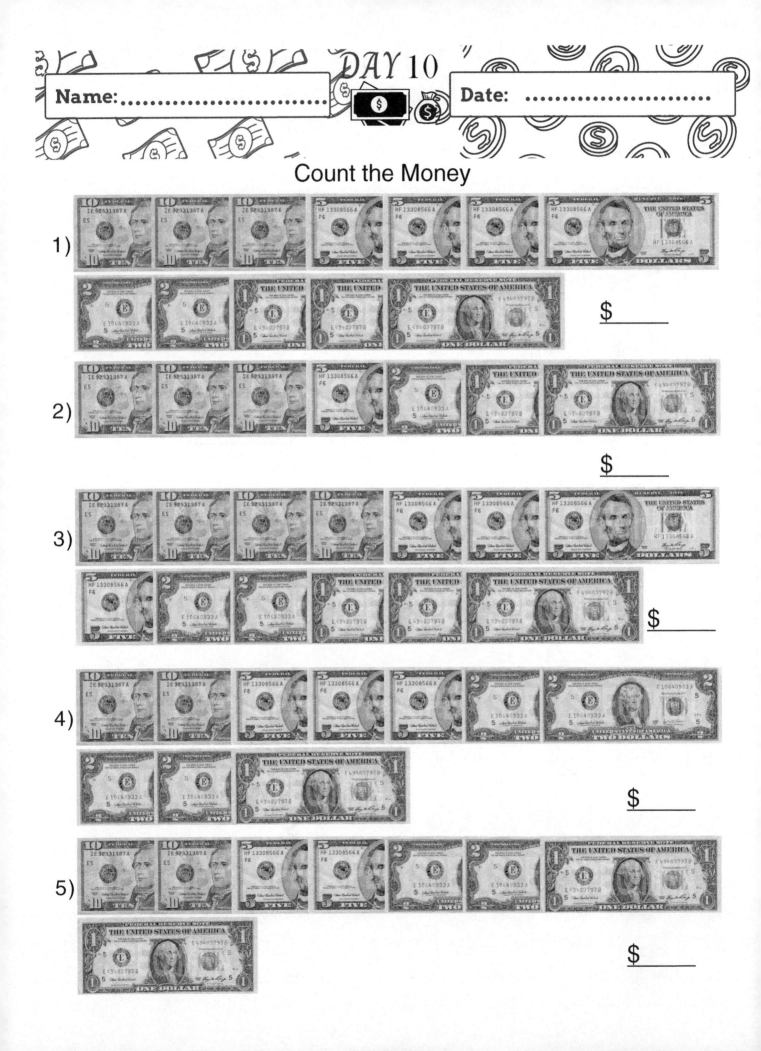

1) $ _____

2) $ _____

3) $ _____

4) $ _____

5) $ _____

Name: ....

Date: ....

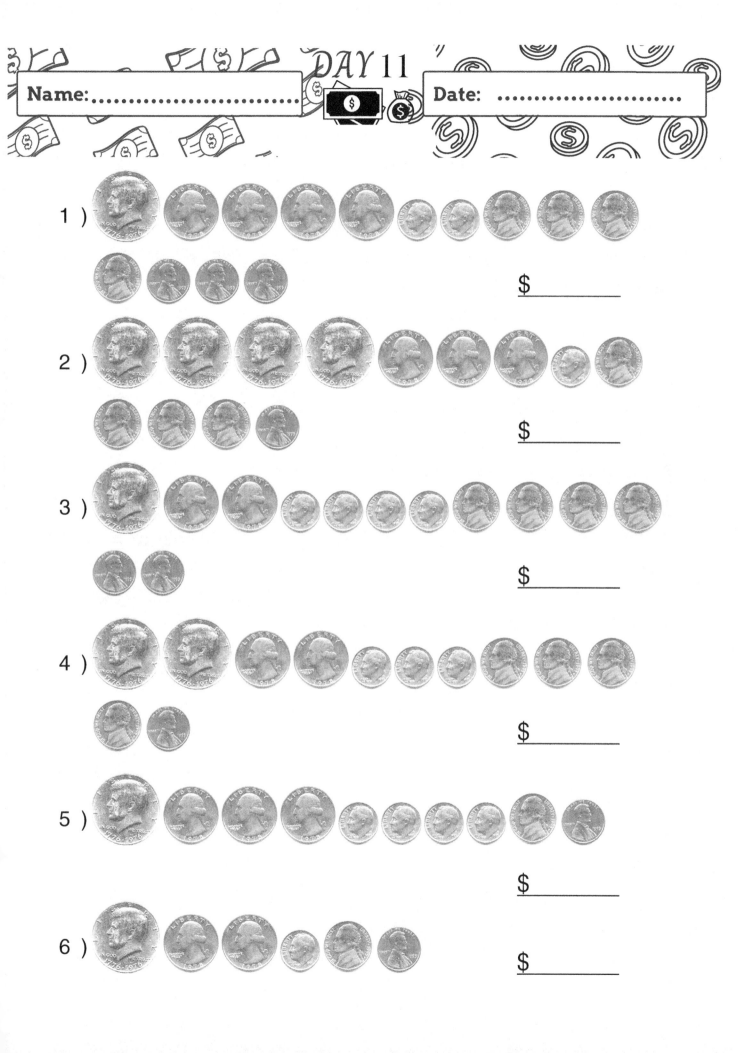

1) $ _____

2) $ _____

3) $ _____

4) $ _____

5) $ _____

6) $ _____

Name: .... **Date:** ....

Count the Money

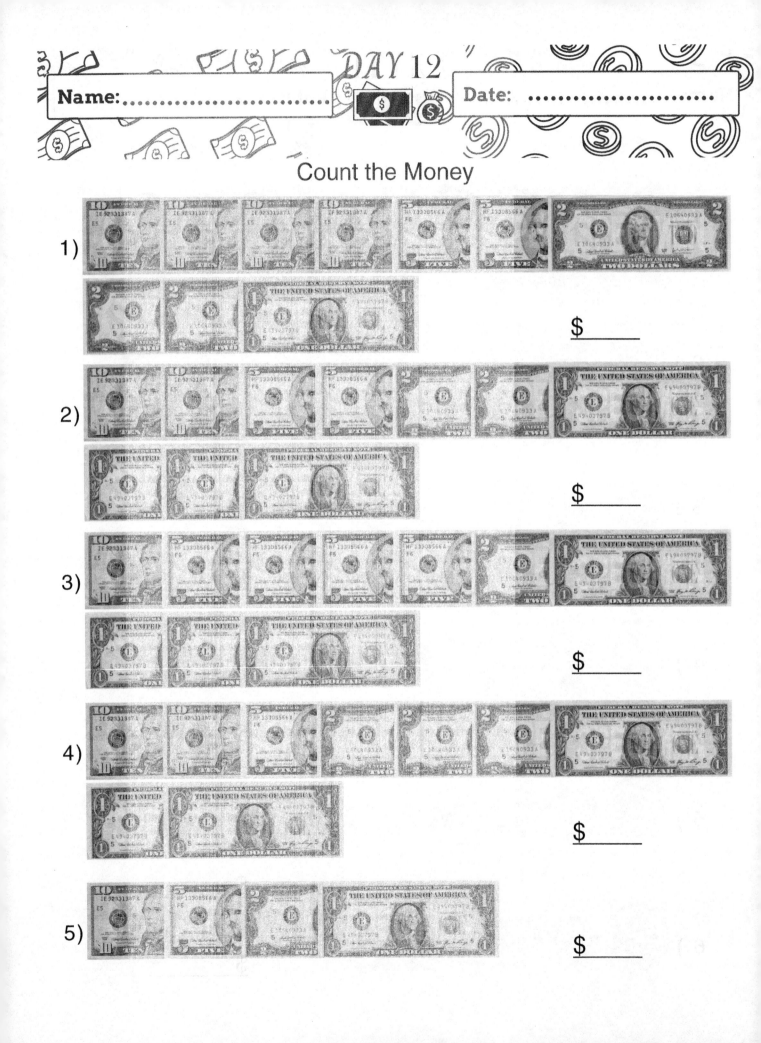

1) $ _____

2) $ _____

3) $ _____

4) $ _____

5) $ _____

Name:................................

Date: ....

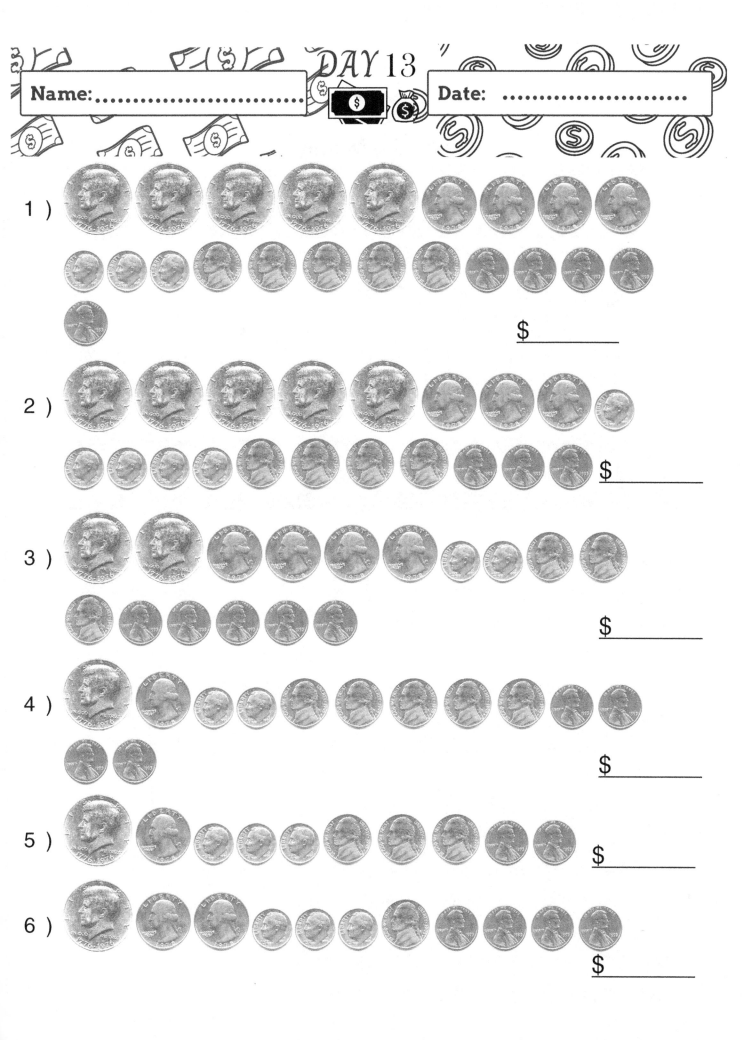

1) $ _____

2) $ _____

3) $ _____

4) $ _____

5) $ _____

6) $ _____

Name:.............................

Date: ....

Count the Money

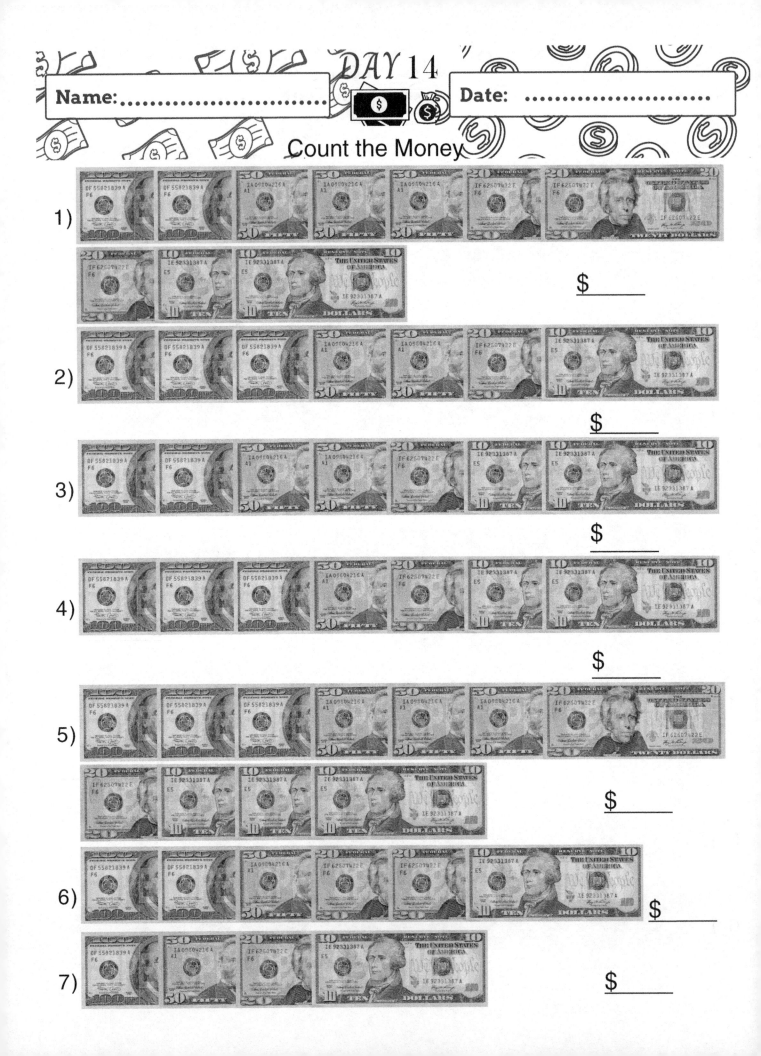

1) $ _____

2) $ _____

3) $ _____

4) $ _____

5) $ _____

6) $ _____

7) $ _____

Name:............................ $ Date: ....

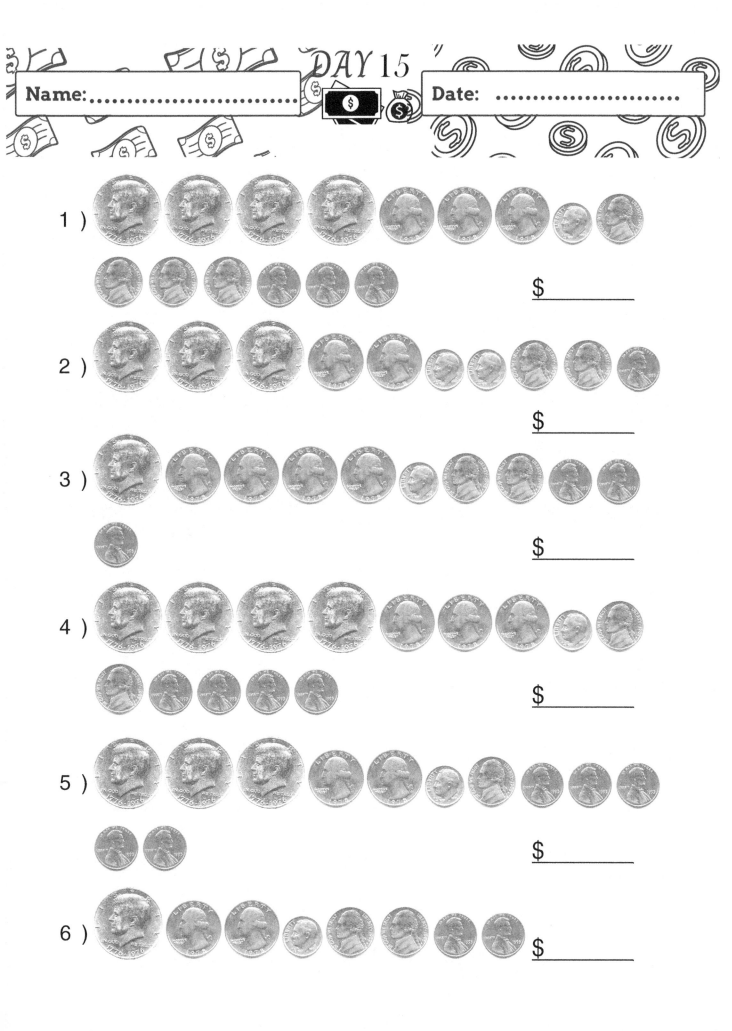

1) $ _____

2) $ _____

3) $ _____

4) $ _____

5) $ _____

6) $ _____

Name:.................................... **Date:** ....

Count the Money

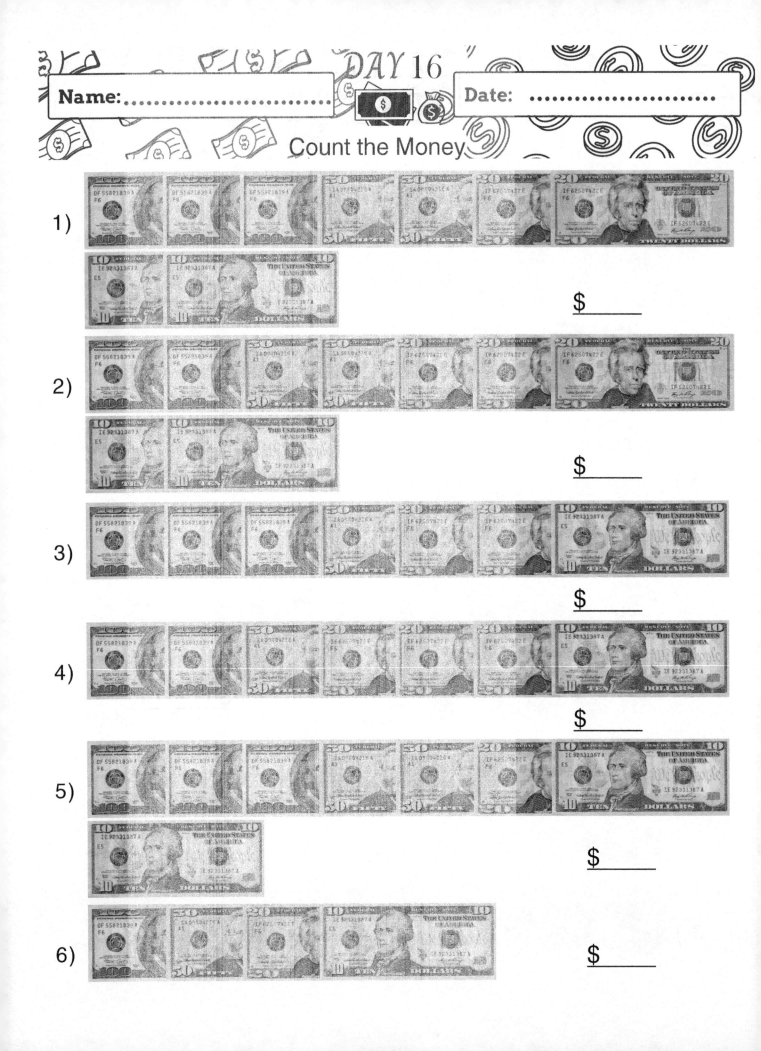

1) $ _____

2) $ _____

3) $ _____

4) $ _____

5) $ _____

6) $ _____

Name:................................ 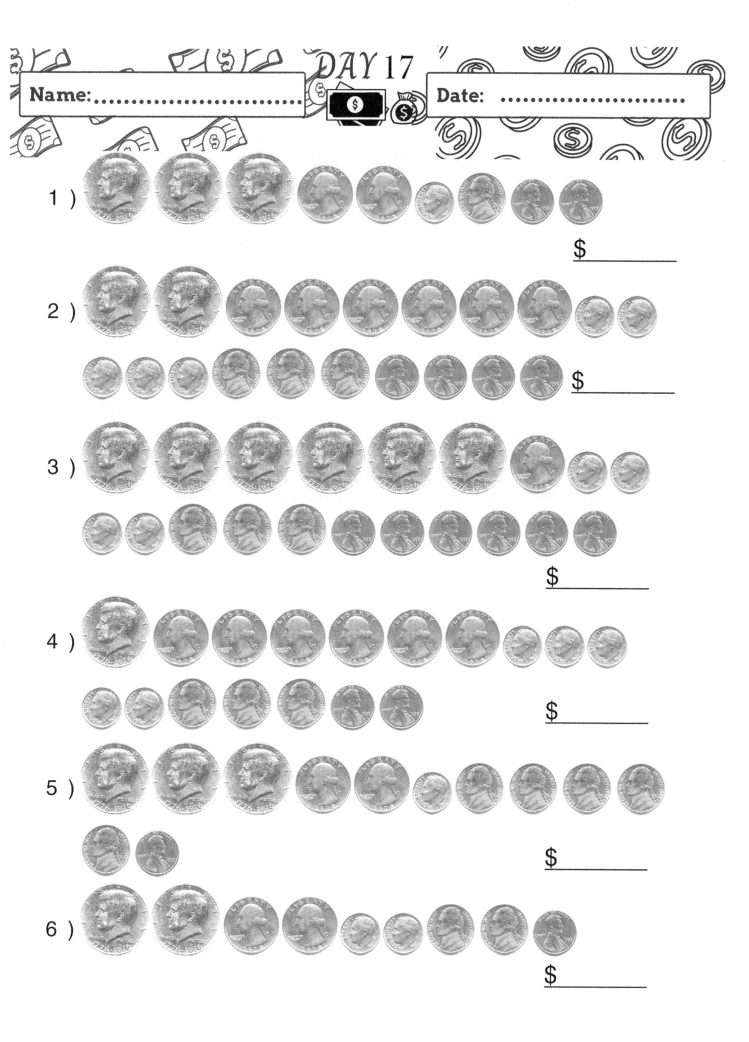 Date: ....

1)

$ _____

2)

$ _____

3)

$ _____

4)

$ _____

5)

$ _____

6)

$ _____

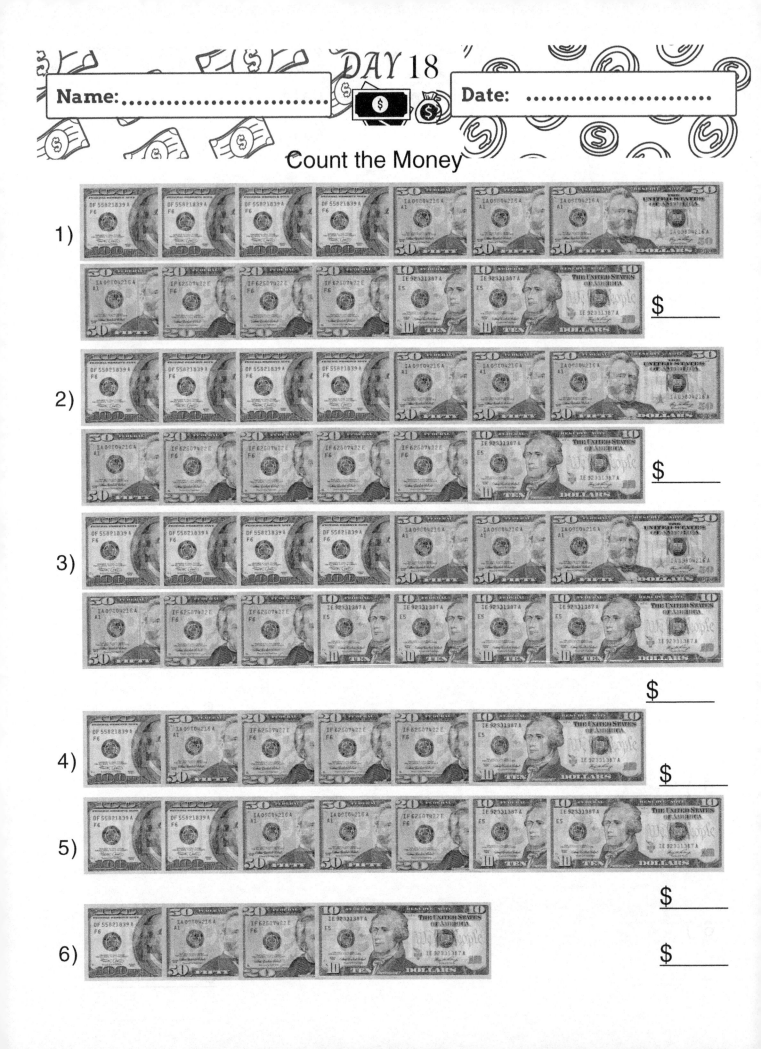

Name: ....

Date: ....

Count the Money

1) $_____

2) $_____

3) $_____

4) $_____

5) $_____

6) $_____

Name: ....

Date: ....

1)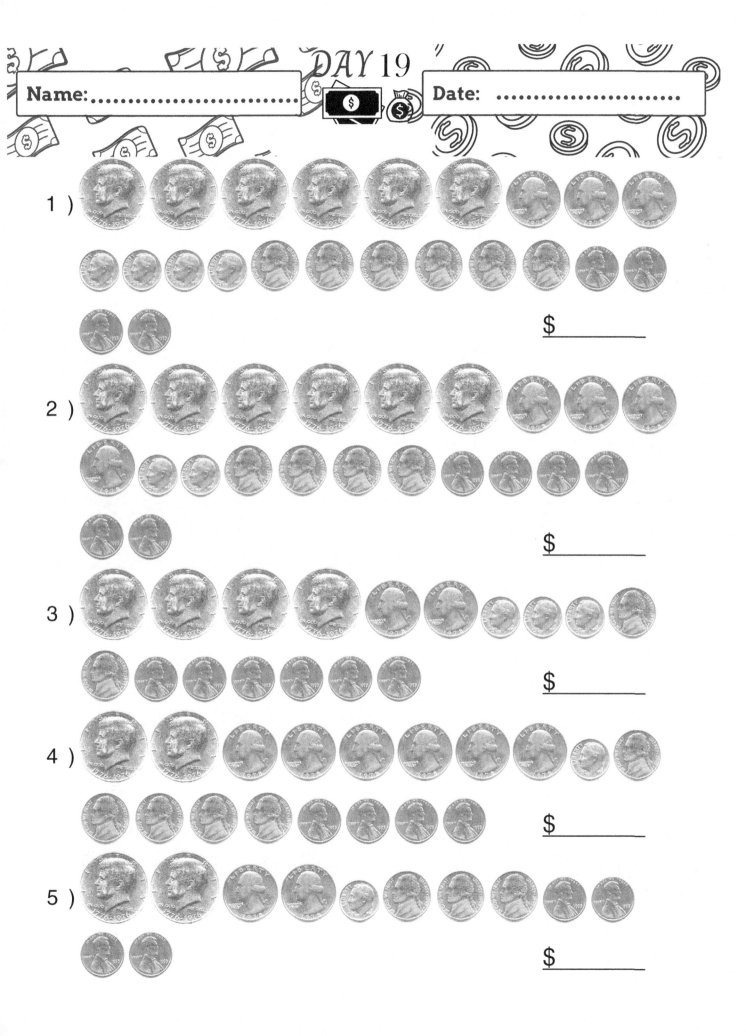

$ _____

2)

$ _____

3)

$ _____

4)

$ _____

5)

$ _____

Name:.............................

Date: ....

Count the Money

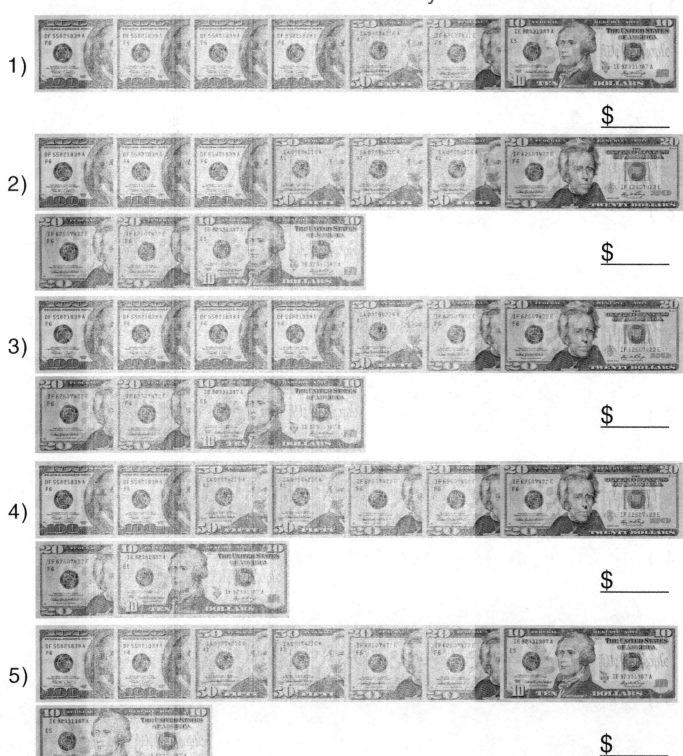

1) $ _____

2) $ _____

3) $ _____

4) $ _____

5) $ _____

DAY 21

Name:................................

Date: ....

Count the Money

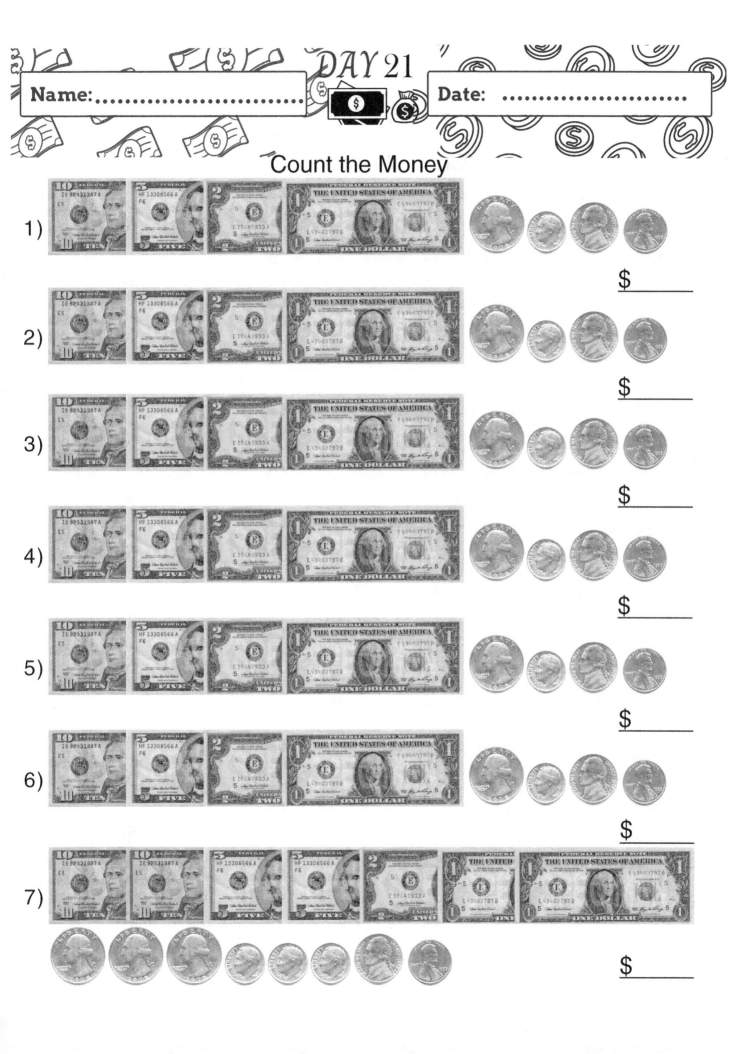

1) $ _____

2) $ _____

3) $ _____

4) $ _____

5) $ _____

6) $ _____

7) $ _____

Count the Money

1)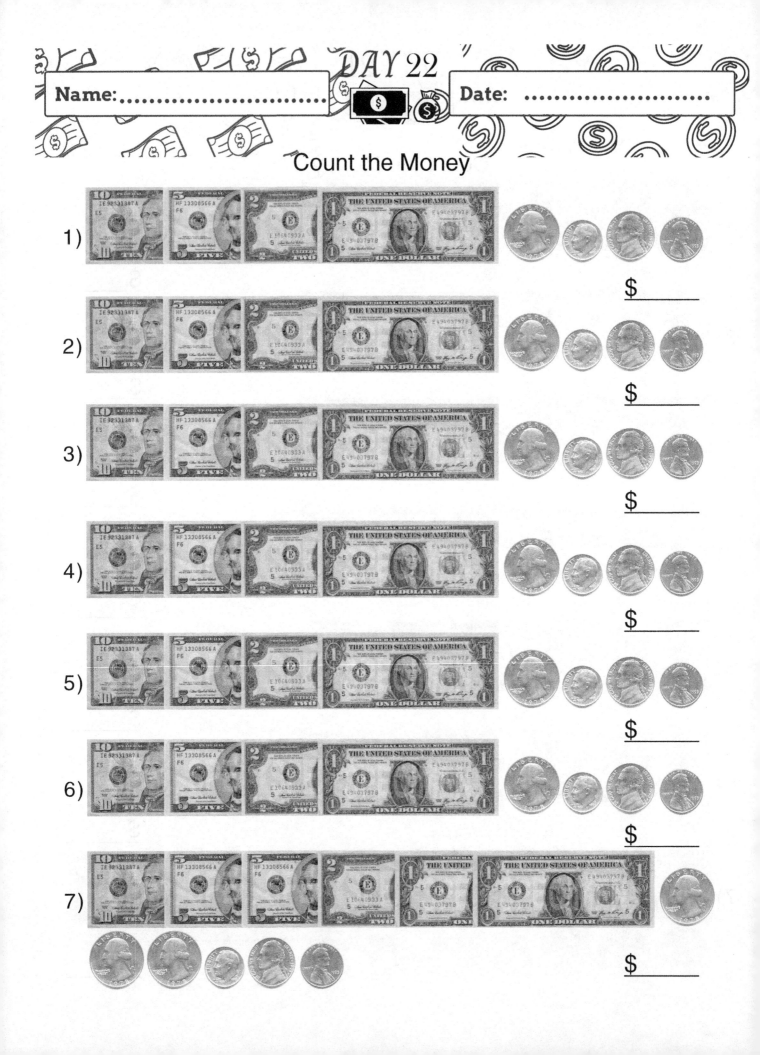

$ _____

2)

$ _____

3)

$ _____

4)

$ _____

5)

$ _____

6)

$ _____

7)

$ _____

Name: ....

Date: ....

Count the Money

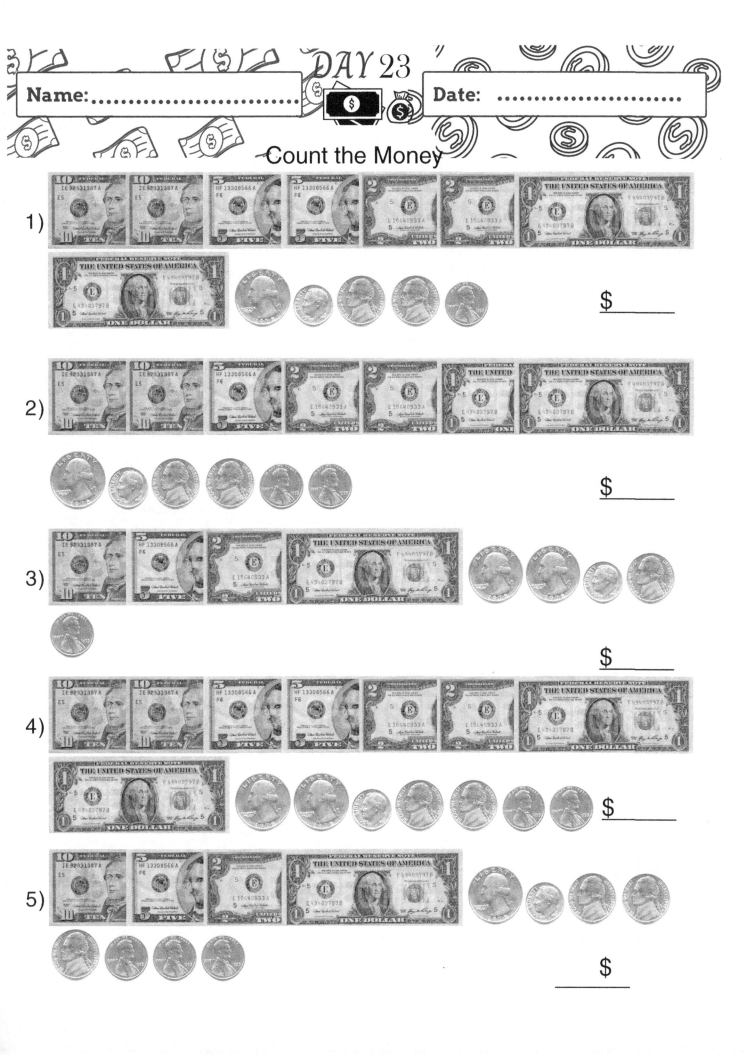

1) $ _____

2) $ _____

3) $ _____

4) $ _____

5) $ _____

Count the Money

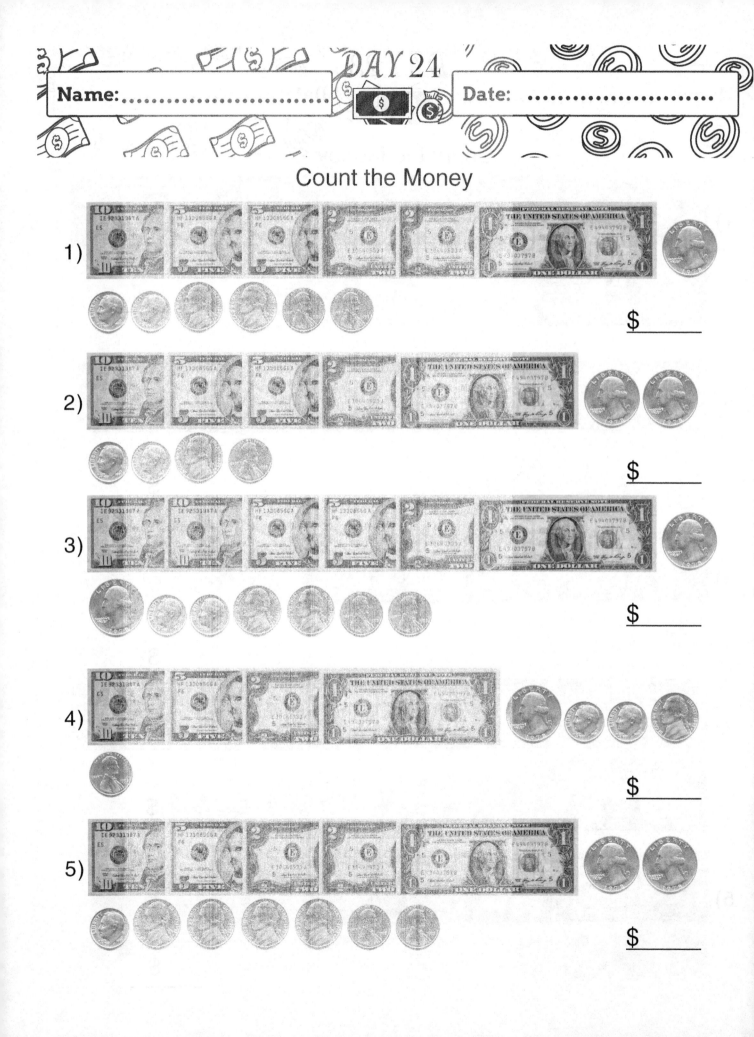

1) $ _____

2) $ _____

3) $ _____

4) $ _____

5) $ _____

Name: ....

Date: ....

Name:............................

Date: ....

Count the Money

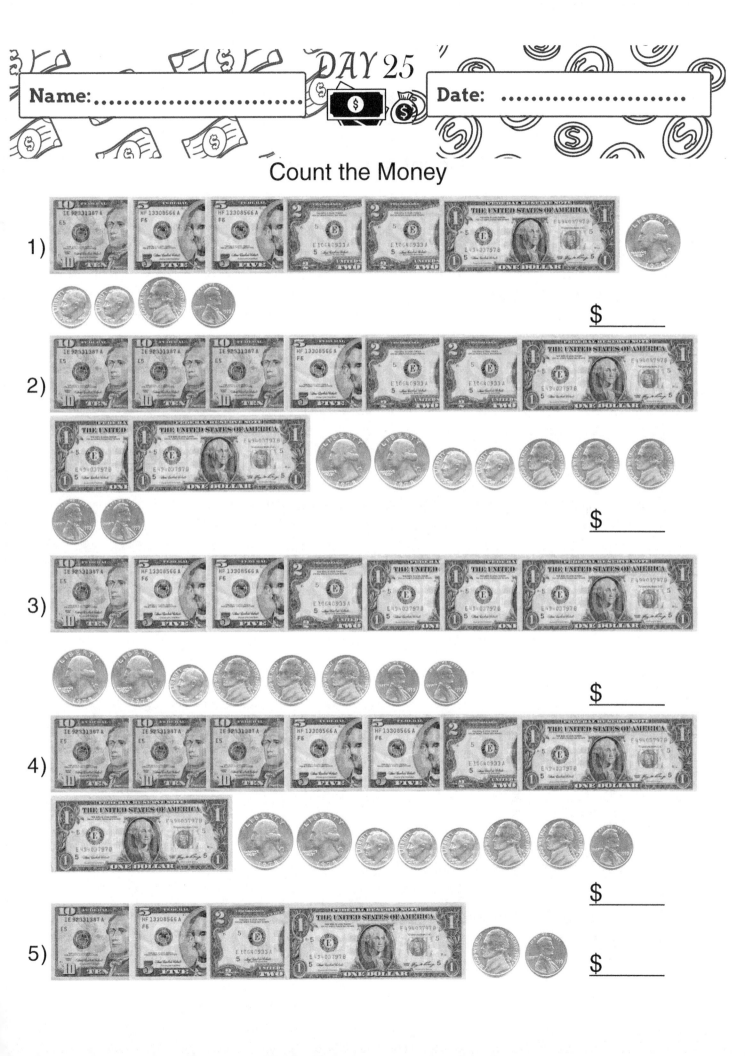

1) $ _____

2) $ _____

3) $ _____

4) $ _____

5) $ _____

Name: .... **Date:** ....

Count the Money

1) 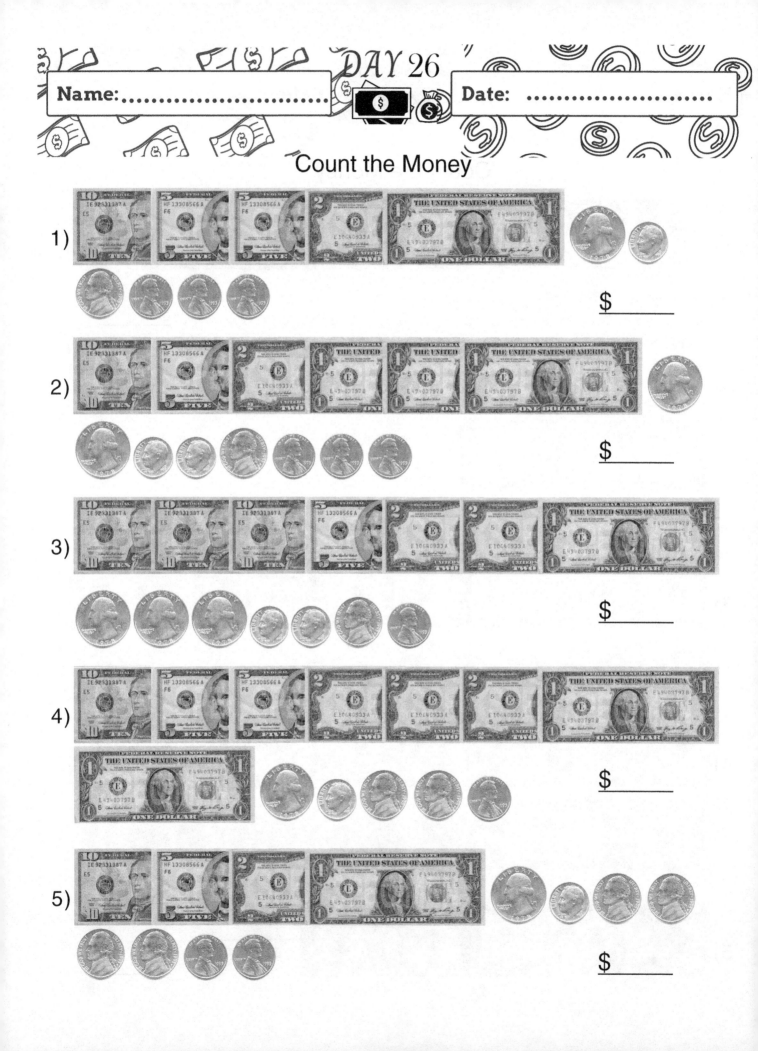 $ _____

2) $ _____

3) $ _____

4) $ _____

5) $ _____

DAY 27

Count the Money

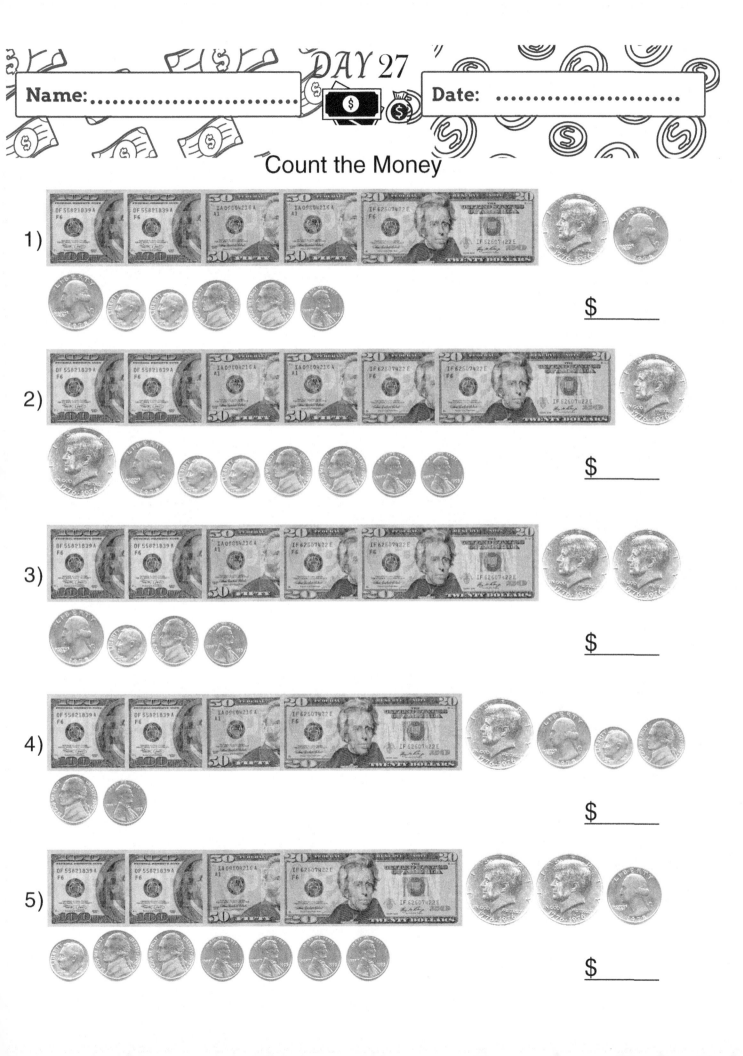

1) $ _____

2) $ _____

3) $ _____

4) $ _____

5) $ _____

Name:................................ Date: ....

Count the Money

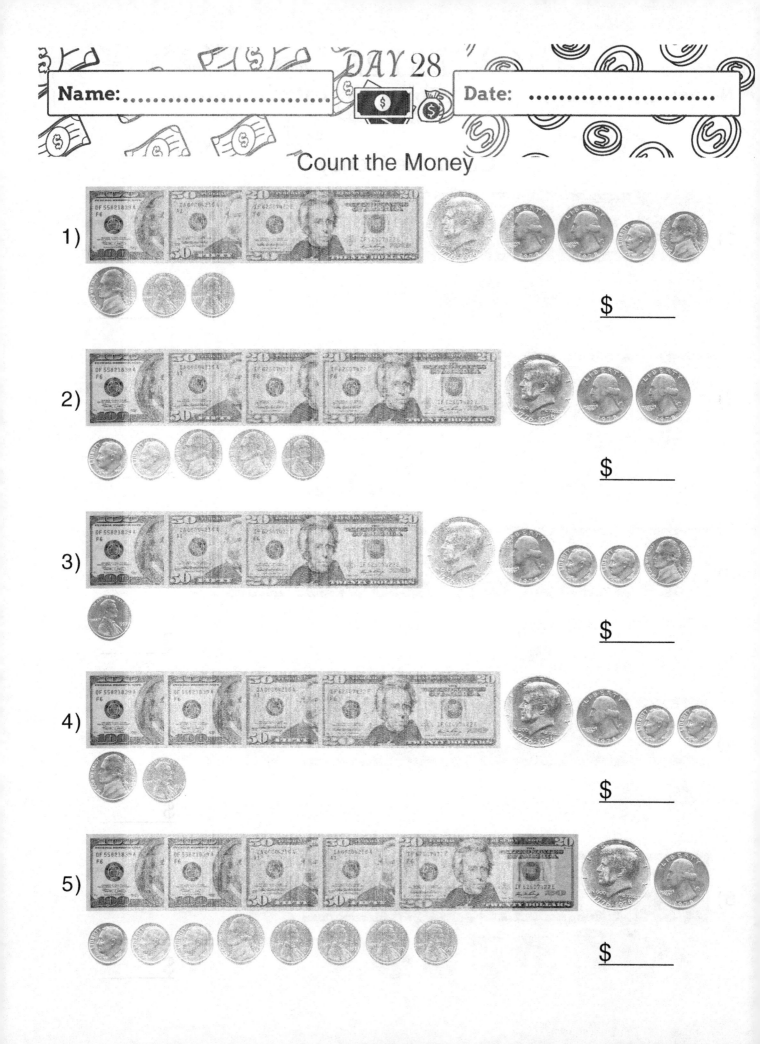

1) $ _____

2) $ _____

3) $ _____

4) $ _____

5) $ _____

Name: ....

Date: ....

Count the Money

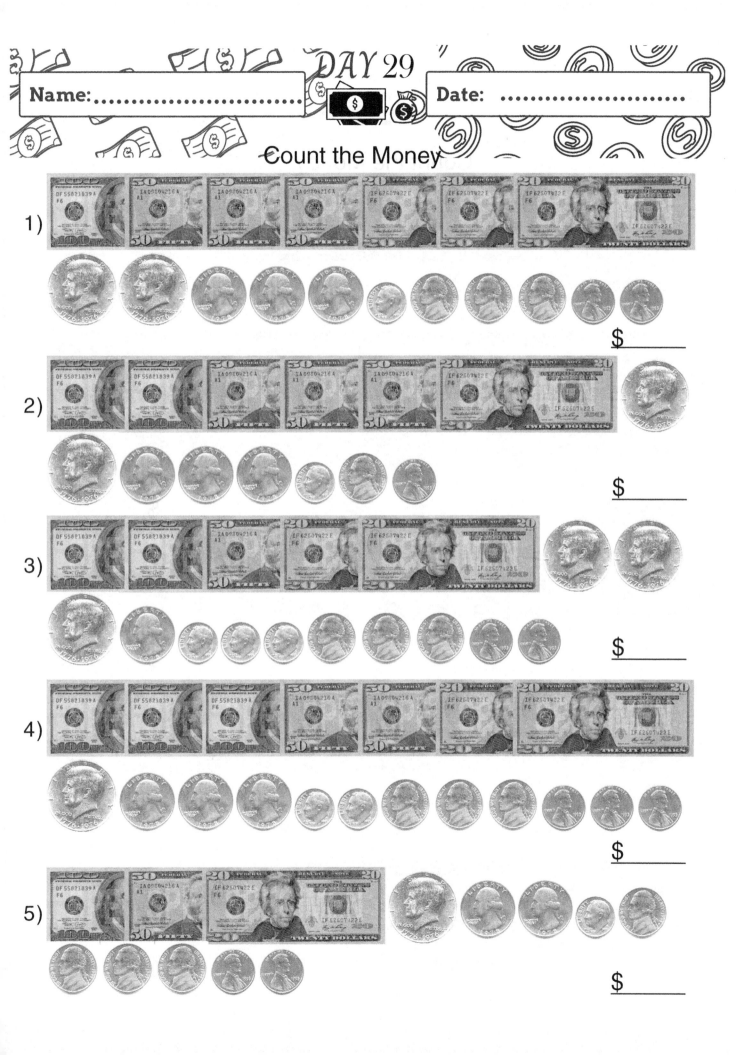

1) $ _____

2) $ _____

3) $ _____

4) $ _____

5) $ _____

Name:...........................

Date: ....

Count the Money

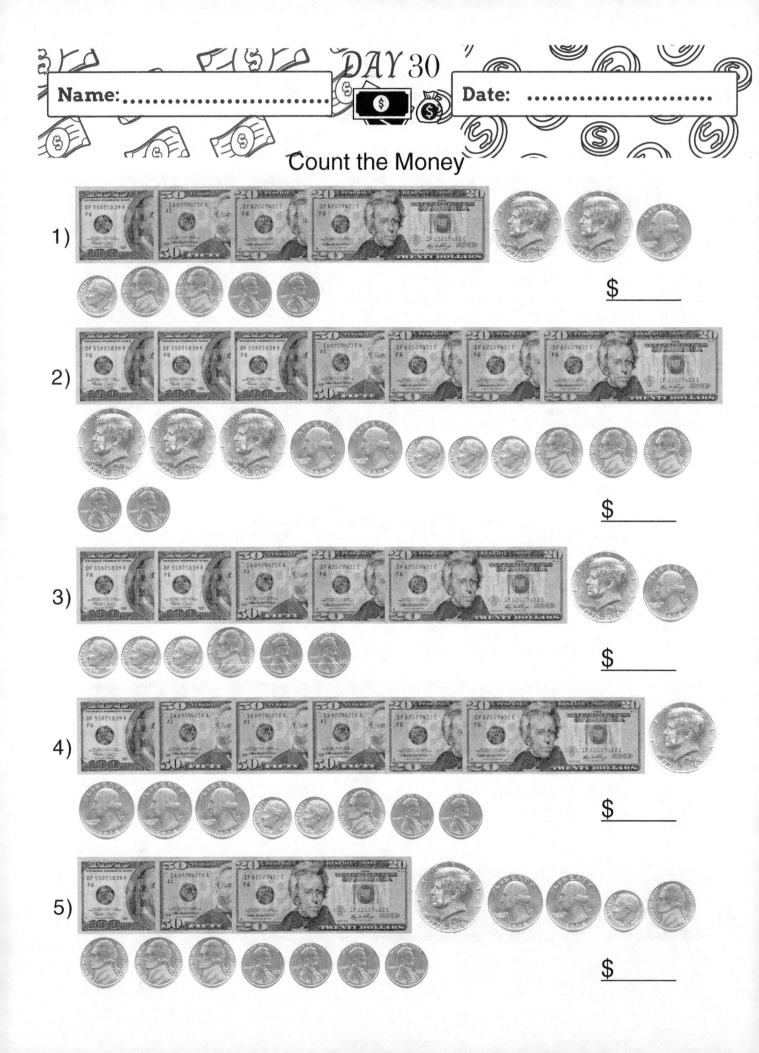

1) $ _____

2) $ _____

3) $ _____

4) $ _____

5) $ _____

DAY 31

Write the Correct Comparison Symbol (>, < or =) in Each Box

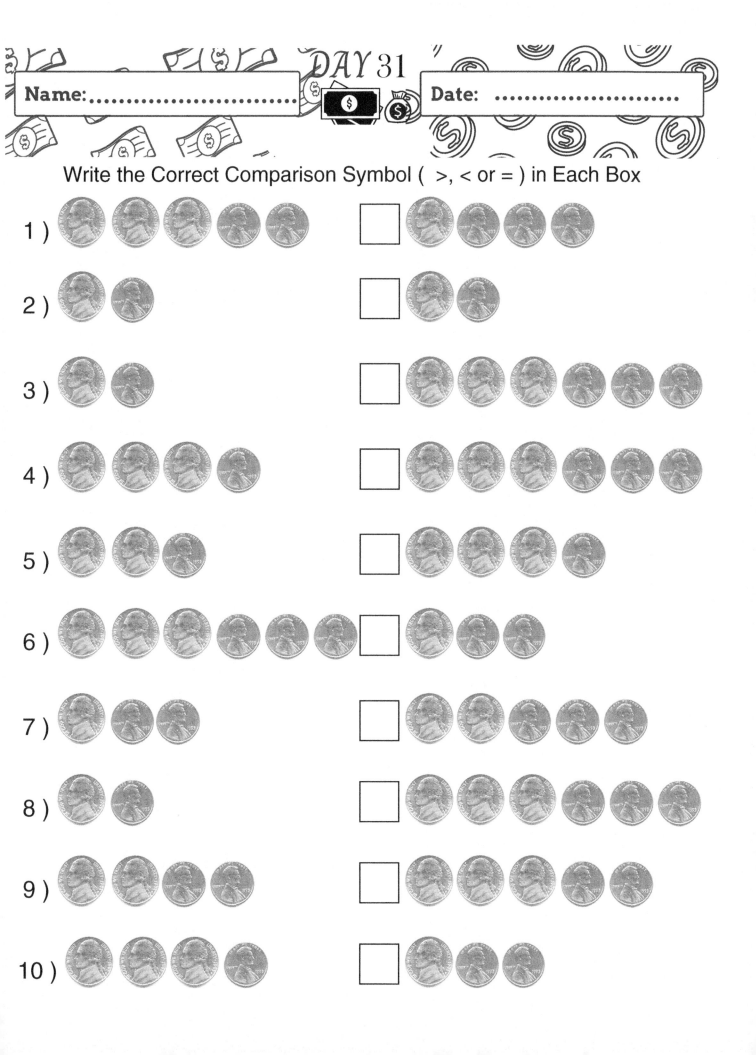

1)
2)
3)
4)
5)
6)
7)
8)
9)
10)

Name: .... **Date:** ....

Write the Correct Comparison Symbol (>, < or =) in Each Box

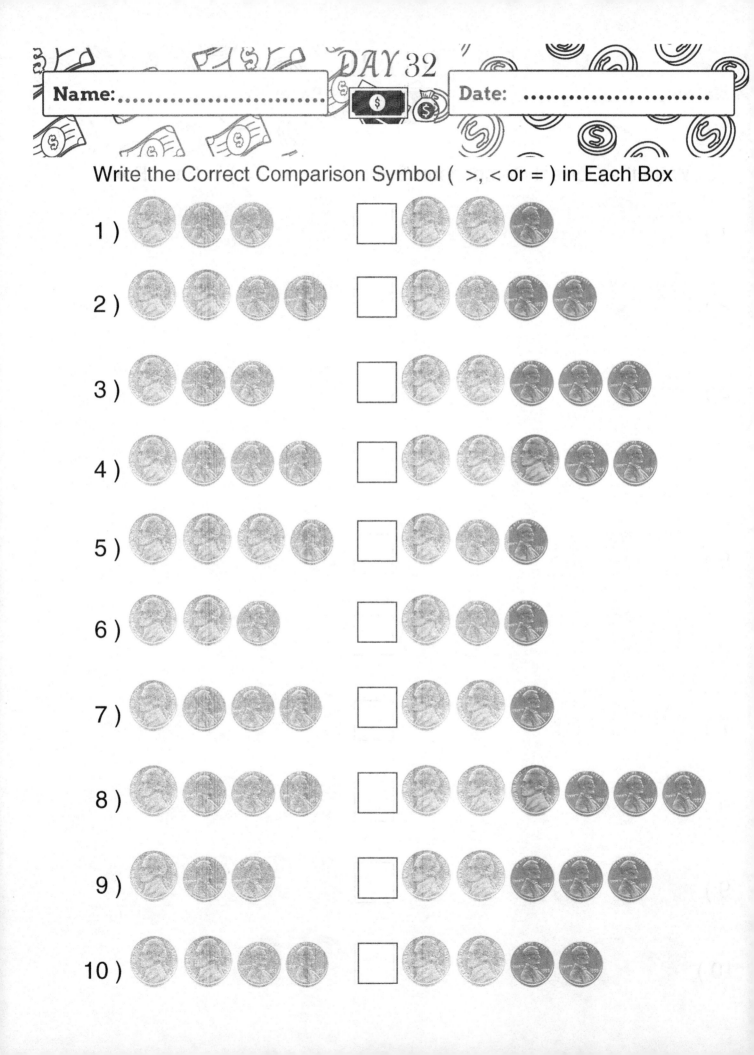

1)

2)

3)

4)

5)

6)

7)

8)

9)

10)

Name:............................ Date: ....

Write the Correct Comparison Symbol (>, < or =) in Each Box

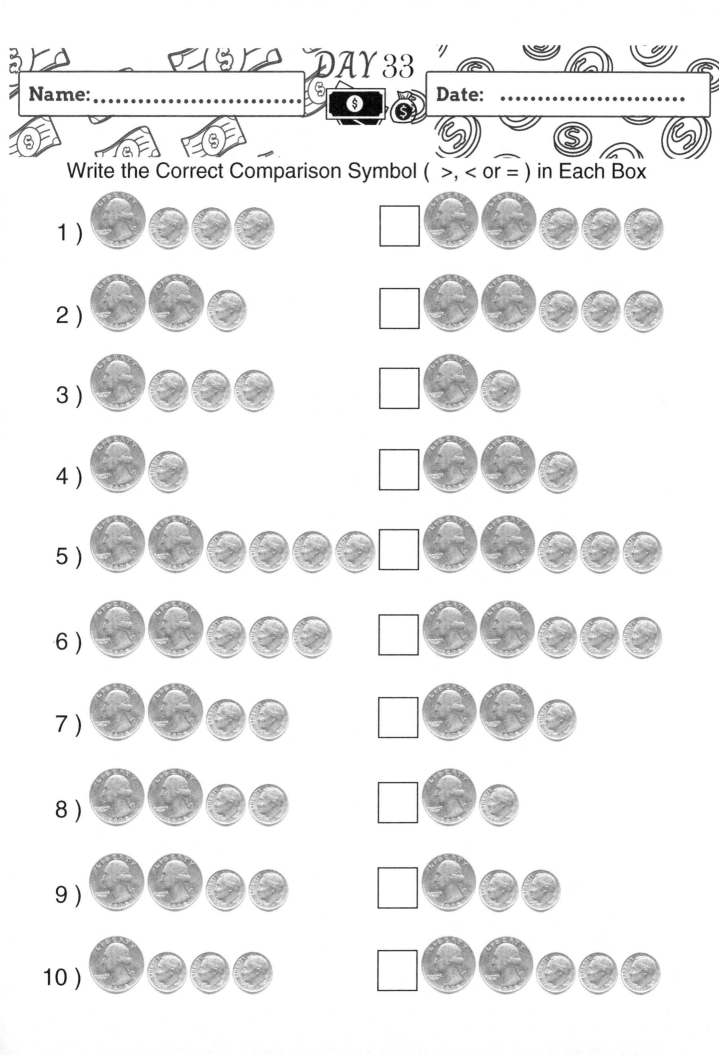

1)

2)

3)

4)

5)

6)

7)

8)

9)

10)

Name:..........................   Date: ....

Write the Correct Comparison Symbol (>, < or =) in Each Box

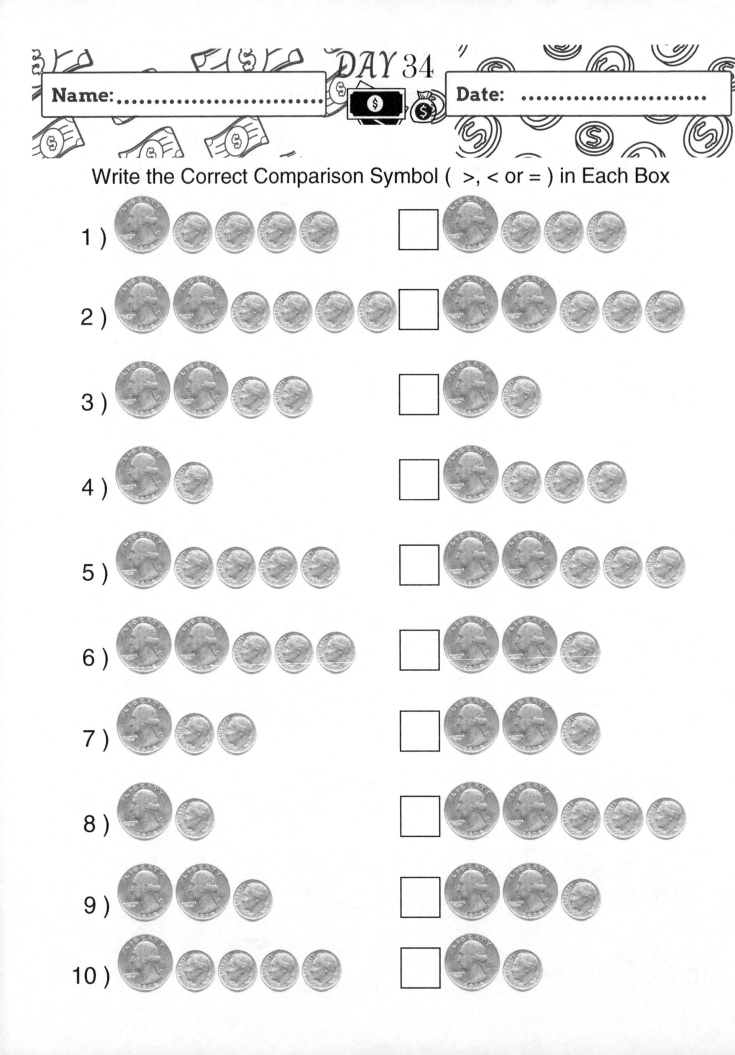

1)

2)

3)

4)

5)

6)

7)

8)

9)

10)

Name:............................   Date: ....

Write the Correct Comparison Symbol (>, < or =) in Each Box

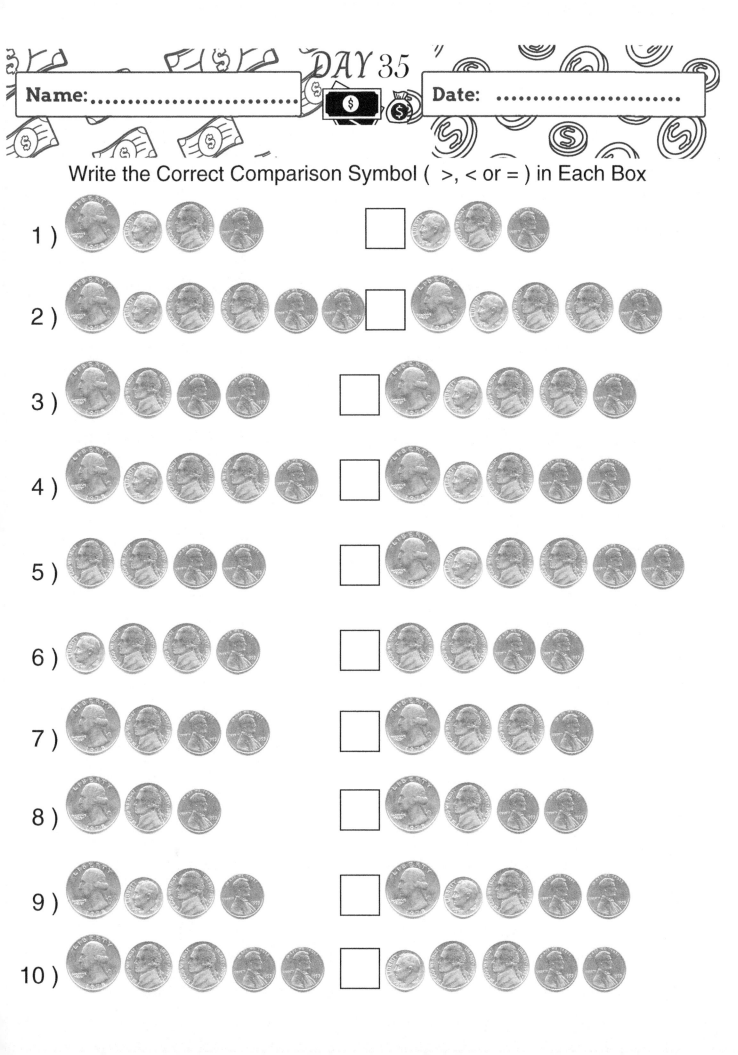

Name: ....

Date: ....

Write the Correct Comparison Symbol (>, < or =) in Each Box

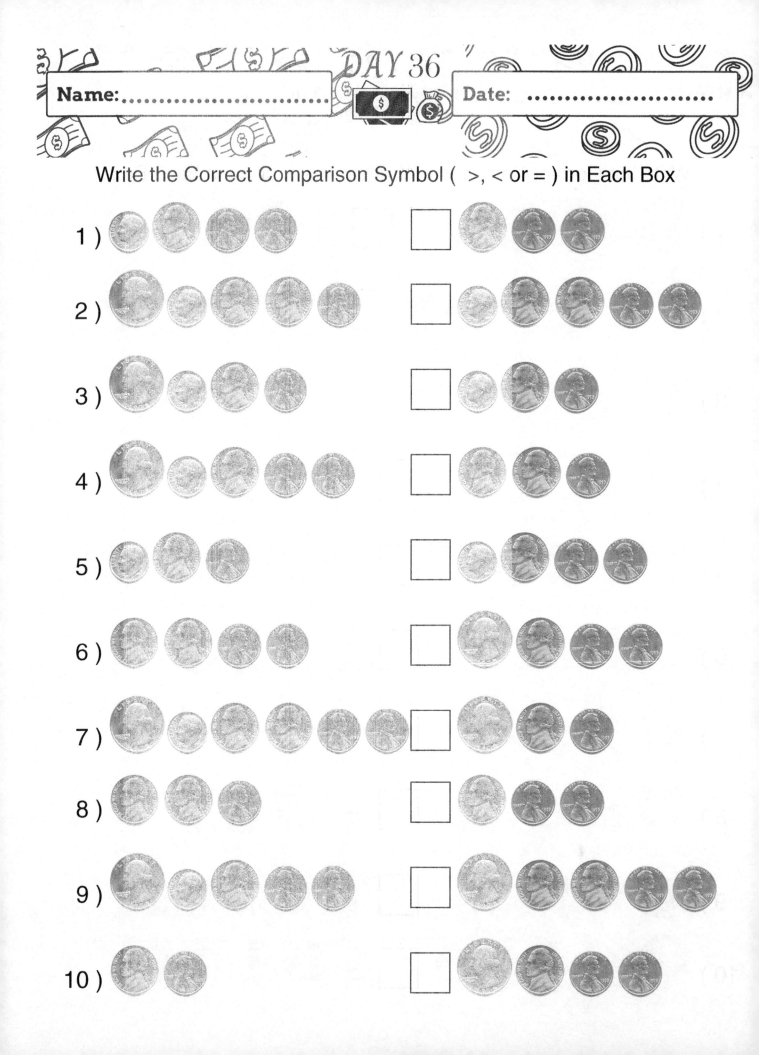

1)

2)

3)

4)

5)

6)

7)

8)

9)

10)

Name:..........................

Date: ....

Write the Correct Comparison Symbol (>, < or =) in Each Box

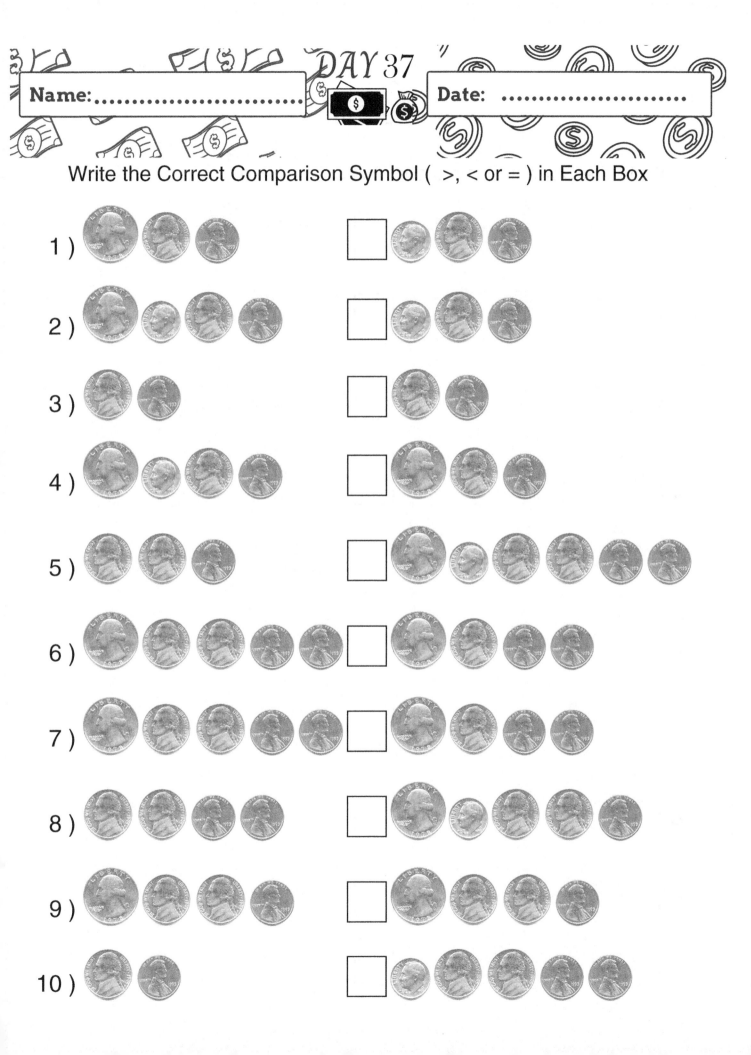

Name: ....

Date: ....

Write the Correct Comparison Symbol (>, < or =) in Each Box

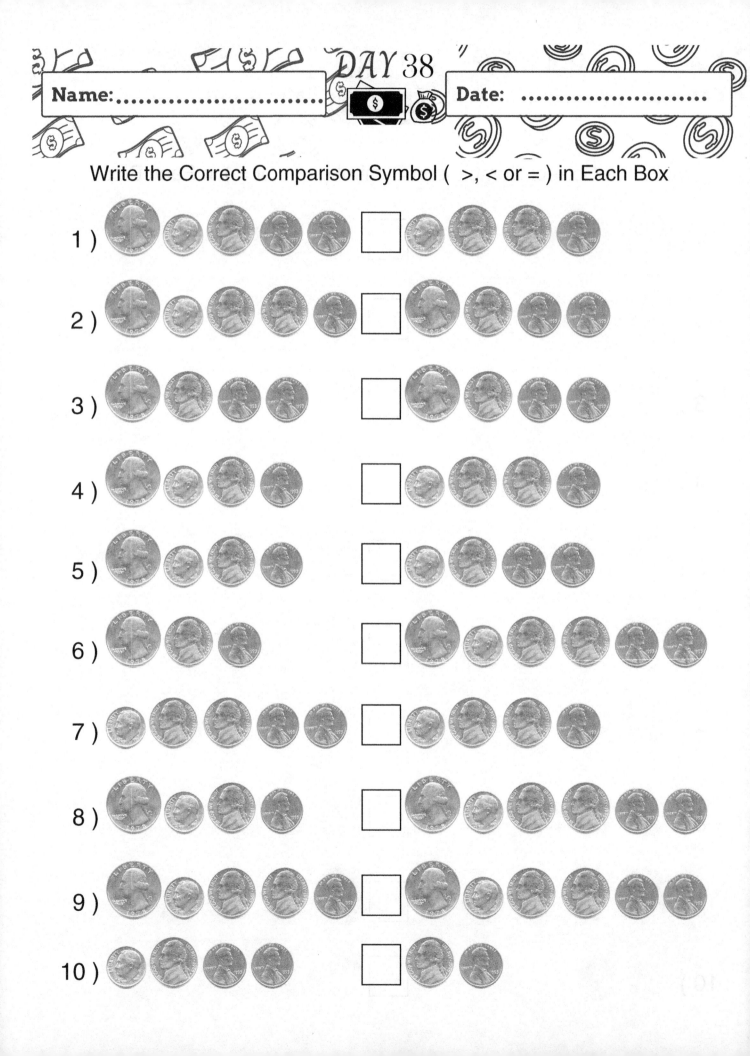

Name: ....   **Date:** ....

Write the Correct Comparison Symbol (>, < or =) in Each Box

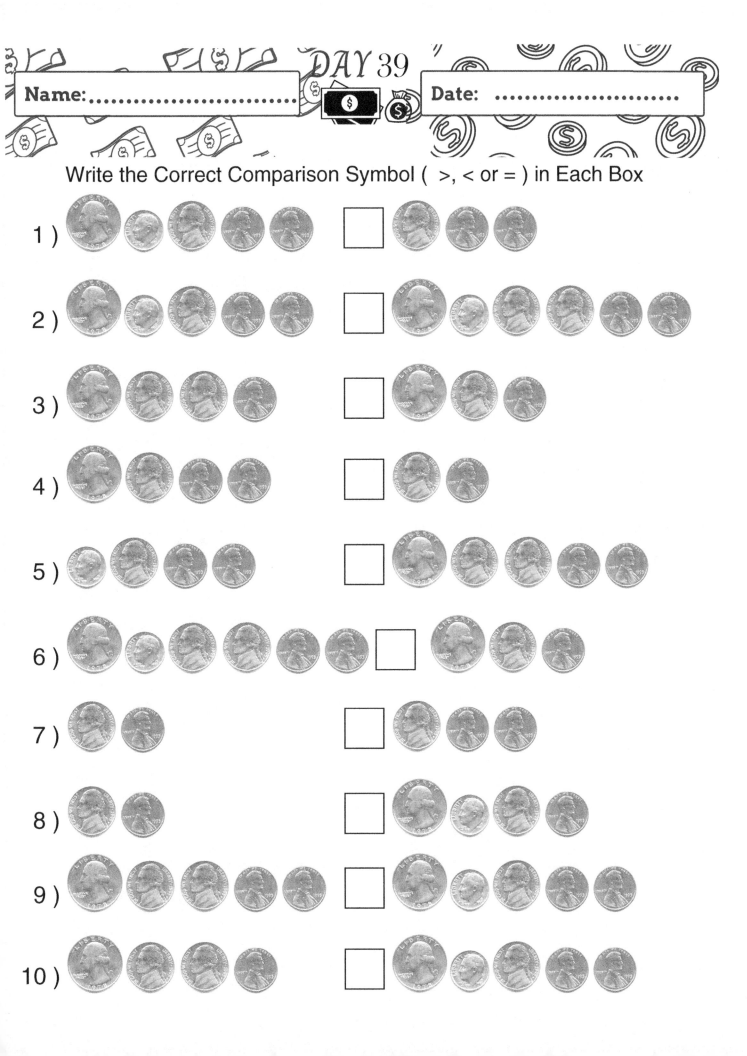

Name:...................................

Date: ....

Write the Correct Comparison Symbol (>, < or =) in Each Box

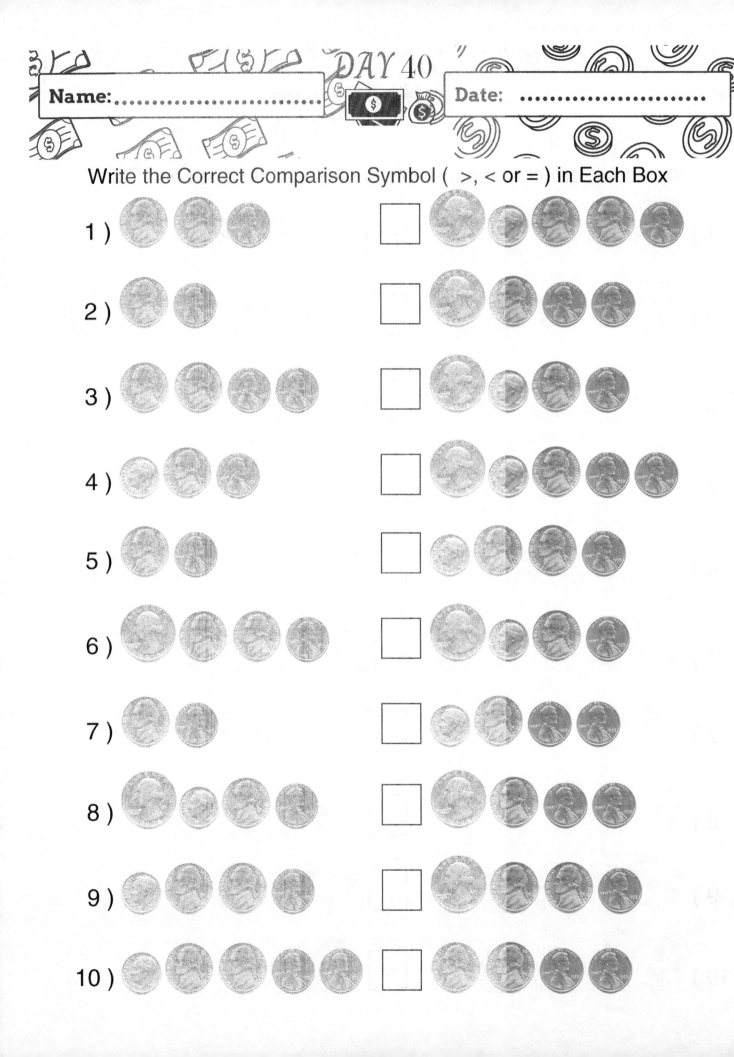

Name: ....

Date: ....

Label the   Penny with a P   Nickel with a N

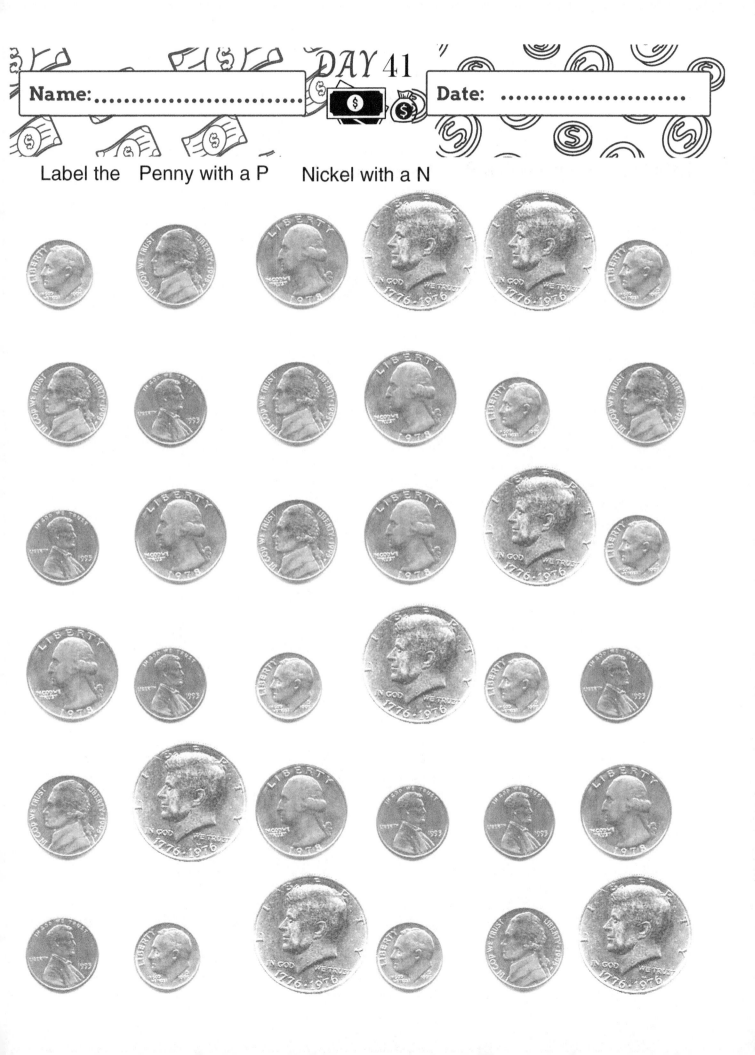

Name:..........................

Date: ....

Label the   Penny with a P   Nickel with a N

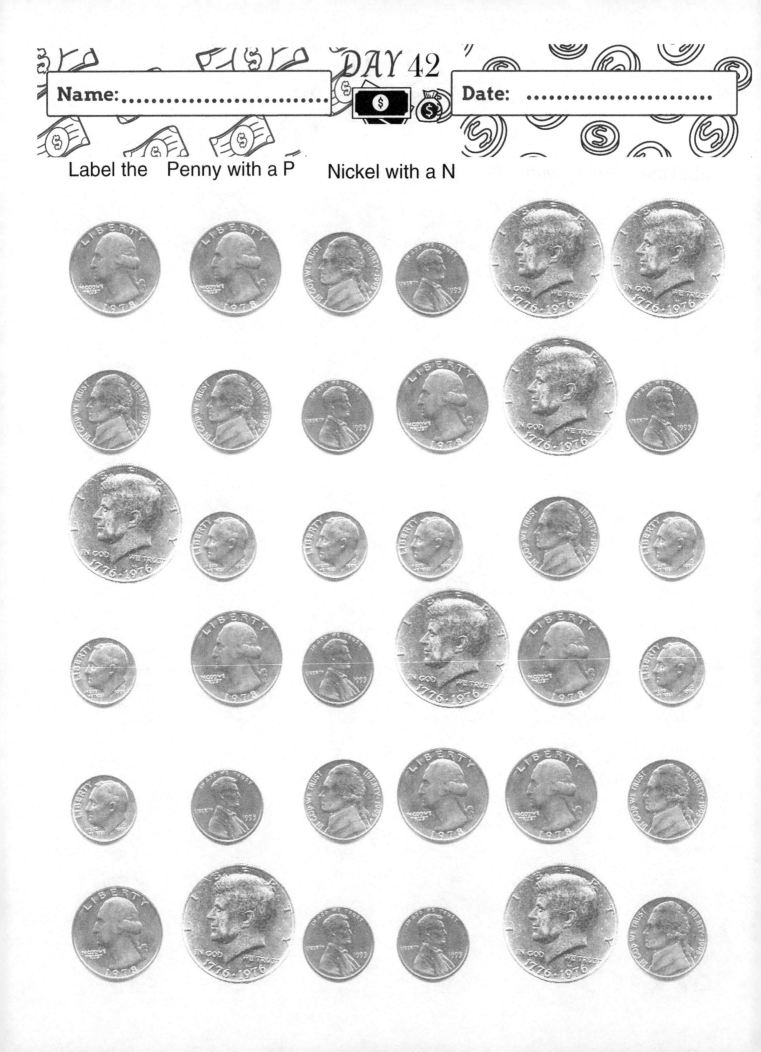

Label the   Dime with a D   Quarter with a Q   Half Dollar with a H

DAY 44

Name:.................................

Date: ....

Label the   Dime with a D   Quarter with a Q   Half Dollar with a H

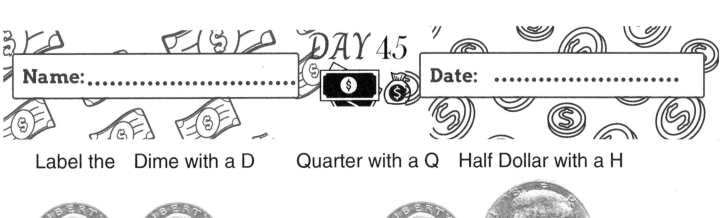

Label the   Dime with a D   Quarter with a Q   Half Dollar with a H

Name:..........................

Date: ....

Label the   Penny with a P   Nickel with a N   Dime with a D   Quarter with a Q
Half Dollar with a H

Name:.............................

Date: ....

Label the   Penny with a P   Nickel with a N   Dime with a D   Quarter with a Q
Half Dollar with a H

Name:......................... **Date:** ....

Label the Penny with a P Nickel with a N Dime with a D Quarter with a Q
Half Dollar with a H

Label the   Penny with a P   Nickel with a N   Dime with a D   Quarter with a Q

Half Dollar with a H

DAY 50

Name: ....

Date: ....

Label the   Penny with a P   Nickel with a N   Dime with a D   Quarter with a Q
Half Dollar with a H

Name: ....

Date: ....

Write the checks out for the purchases.

1) You purchase food at Olive Garden on January 20, 2015 for $15.77.

Your Name Here   **100**
2345 Your Street
Your City, Your State 12345   DATE _____   47-352/849
                                                                              3467

PAY TO THE
ORDER OF _____ I $ _____

_____ DOLLARS 🔒 Security features
                                                            are included
                                                            Details on back

PI-MATH BANK
   Mathematics USA

Memo _____ Signature _____ MP

⑆052341678⑆ 5125497653 ⑈ 100

2) You purchase groceries at Walmart on April 3, 2015 for $149.96.

Your Name Here   **101**
2345 Your Street
Your City, Your State 12345   DATE _____   47-352/849
                                                                              3467

PAY TO THE
ORDER OF _____ I $ _____

_____ DOLLARS 🔒 Security features
                                                            are included
                                                            Details on back

PI-MATH BANK
   Mathematics USA

Memo _____ Signature _____ MP

⑆052341678⑆ 5125497653 ⑈ 101

Write the checks out for the purchases.

1) You purchase groceries at Food Lion on April 11, 2015 for $78.74.

Your Name Here	**100**
2345 Your Street	
Your City, Your State 12345	47-352/849
	3467
DATE _____	
PAY TO THE	
ORDER OF _____	$ _____
_____ DOLLARS 🔒	Security features are included Details on back.
PI-MATH BANK	
Mathematics USA	
Memo _____ Signature _____	MP

⑆052341678⑈ 5125497653⑈ 100

2) You purchase food at Burger King on June 23, 2015 for $14.67.

Your Name Here	**101**
2345 Your Street	
Your City, Your State 12345	47-352/849
	3467
DATE _____	
PAY TO THE	
ORDER OF _____	$ _____
_____ DOLLARS 🔒	Security features are included Details on back.
PI-MATH BANK	
Mathematics USA	
Memo _____ Signature _____	MP

⑆052341678⑈ 5125497653⑈ 101

Write the checks out for the purchases.

1) You purchase food at McDonald's on July 10, 2015 for $13.81.

Your Name Here   **200**
2345 Your Street
Your City, Your State 12345   DATE _____   47-352/849
                                                                              3467

PAY TO THE
ORDER OF _____ | $ [_____]

_____ DOLLARS 🔒 Security features
                                                        are included
                                                        Details on back

PI-MATH BANK
   Mathematics USA

Memo _____   Signature _____   MP

⑈052341678⑈ 5125497653 ⑈ 200

2) You purchase groceries at Albertson on April 26, 2015 for $147.52.

Your Name Here   **201**
2345 Your Street
Your City, Your State 12345   DATE _____   47-352/849
                                                                              3467

PAY TO THE
ORDER OF _____ | $ [_____]

_____ DOLLARS 🔒 Security features
                                                        are included
                                                        Details on back

PI-MATH BANK
   Mathematics USA

Memo _____   Signature _____   MP

⑈052341678⑈ 5125497653 ⑈ 201

Write the checks out for the purchases.

1) You purchase food at Taco Bell on April 20, 2015 for $17.28.

Your Name Here   **200**
2345 Your Street
Your City, Your State 12345   DATE _____   47-352/849
                                                                        3467

PAY TO THE
ORDER OF _____ | $ _____

_____ DOLLARS 🔒 Security features are included. Details on back.

PI-MATH BANK
   Mathematics USA

Memo _____ Signature _____ MP

⑆052341678⑆ 5125497653⑈ 200

2) You purchase groceries at Kroger on February 2, 2015 for $66.86.

Your Name Here   **201**
2345 Your Street
Your City, Your State 12345   DATE _____   47-352/849
                                                                         3467

PAY TO THE
ORDER OF _____ | $ _____

_____ DOLLARS 🔒 Security features are included. Details on back.

PI-MATH BANK
   Mathematics USA

Memo _____ Signature _____ MP

⑆052341678⑆ 5125497653⑈ 201

Write the checks out for the purchases.

1) You purchase groceries at Food Lion on April 4, 2015 for $47.75.

Your Name Here   **1000**
2345 Your Street
Your City, Your State 12345   DATE _____   47-352/849
3467

PAY TO THE
ORDER OF _____ $ [   ]

_____ DOLLARS 🔒 Security features are included Details on back.

PI-MATH BANK
   Mathematics USA

Memo _____ Signature _____ MP

⑆052341678⑆ 5125497653⑈ 1000

2) You purchase food at Taco Bell on January 16, 2015 for $10.24.

Your Name Here   **1001**
2345 Your Street
Your City, Your State 12345   DATE _____   47-352/849
3467

PAY TO THE
ORDER OF _____ $ [   ]

_____ DOLLARS 🔒 Security features are included Details on back.

PI-MATH BANK
   Mathematics USA

Memo _____ Signature _____ MP

⑆052341678⑆ 5125497653⑈ 1001

Name: ....   Date: ....

Write the checks out for the purchases.

1) You purchase groceries at ShopRite on August 3, 2015 for $146.26.

	1000
Your Name Here	
2345 Your Street	
Your City, Your State 12345	DATE _____ 47-352/849 3467

PAY TO THE
ORDER OF _____ | $ [   ]

_____ DOLLARS 🔒 Security features are included Details on back

PI-MATH BANK
   Mathematics USA

Memo _____   Signature _____   MP

⑆052341678⑆ 5125497653⑈ 1000

2) You purchase food at Wendy's on April 8, 2015 for $14.18.

	1001
Your Name Here	
2345 Your Street	
Your City, Your State 12345	DATE _____ 47-352/849 3467

PAY TO THE
ORDER OF _____ | $ [   ]

_____ DOLLARS 🔒 Security features are included Details on back

PI-MATH BANK
   Mathematics USA

Memo _____   Signature _____   MP

⑆052341678⑆ 5125497653⑈ 1001

Write the checks out for the purchases.

1) You purchase groceries at Kroger on February 20, 2015 for $134.42.

Your Name Here   **2000**
2345 Your Street
Your City, Your State 12345   DATE _____   47-352/849
                                                          3467

PAY TO THE
ORDER OF _____ | $ _____

_____ DOLLARS 🔒 Security features are included Details on back

PI-MATH BANK
    Mathematics USA

Memo _____ Signature _____ MP

⑆052341678⑆ 5125497653⑇ 2000

2) You purchase food at Olive Garden on April 8, 2015 for $16.85.

Your Name Here   **2001**
2345 Your Street
Your City, Your State 12345   DATE _____   47-352/849
                                                          3467

PAY TO THE
ORDER OF _____ | $ _____

_____ DOLLARS 🔒 Security features are included Details on back

PI-MATH BANK
    Mathematics USA

Memo _____ Signature _____ MP

⑆052341678⑆ 5125497653⑇ 2001

Write the checks out for the purchases.

1) You purchase food at Hardee's on March 9, 2015 for $18.11.

Your Name Here   **2000**
2345 Your Street
Your City, Your State 12345   DATE _____   47-352/849
                                                                      3467

PAY TO THE
ORDER OF _____ | $ [   ]

_____ DOLLARS 🔒 Security features
                                                                are included
                                                                Details on back.

PI-MATH BANK
   Mathematics USA

Memo _____   Signature _____   MP

⑆ 0 5 2 3 4 1 6 7 8 ⑆ 5 1 2 5 4 9 7 6 5 3 ⑈ 2 0 0 0

2) You purchase groceries at Kroger on August 18, 2015 for $83.94.

Your Name Here   **2001**
2345 Your Street
Your City, Your State 12345   DATE _____   47-352/849
                                                                      3467

PAY TO THE
ORDER OF _____ | $ [   ]

_____ DOLLARS 🔒 Security features
                                                                are included
                                                                Details on back.

PI-MATH BANK
   Mathematics USA

Memo _____   Signature _____   MP

⑆ 0 5 2 3 4 1 6 7 8 ⑆ 5 1 2 5 4 9 7 6 5 3 ⑈ 2 0 0 1

Write the checks out for the purchases.

1) You purchase food at McDonald's on May 23, 2015 for $18.34.

Your Name Here   **2000**
2345 Your Street
Your City, Your State 12345   DATE _____   47-352/849
                                                                                        3467

PAY TO THE
ORDER OF _____ | $ [   ]

_____ DOLLARS 🔒 Security features are included Details on back

   PI-MATH BANK
    Mathematics USA

Memo _____ Signature _____ MP

⑆052341678⑆ 5125497653⑈ 2000

2) You purchase groceries at Publix on November 12, 2015 for $167.57.

Your Name Here   **2001**
2345 Your Street
Your City, Your State 12345   DATE _____   47-352/849
                                                                                        3467

PAY TO THE
ORDER OF _____ | $ [   ]

_____ DOLLARS 🔒 Security features are included Details on back

   PI-MATH BANK
    Mathematics USA

Memo _____ Signature _____ MP

⑆052341678⑆ 5125497653⑈ 2001

Write the checks out for the purchases.

1) You purchase groceries at Food Lion on August 6, 2015 for $107.95.

Your Name Here   **2000**
2345 Your Street
Your City, Your State 12345   DATE _____   47-352/849
                                                                 3467

PAY TO THE
ORDER OF _____ | $ [   ]

_____ DOLLARS 🔒 Security features
                                                            are included
                                                            Details on back.

PI-MATH BANK
   Mathematics USA

Memo _____   Signature _____   MP

⑆052341678⑆ 5125497653⑈ 2000

2) You purchase food at Olive Garden on December 11, 2015 for $18.56.

Your Name Here   **2001**
2345 Your Street
Your City, Your State 12345   DATE _____   47-352/849
                                                                 3467

PAY TO THE
ORDER OF _____ | $ [   ]

_____ DOLLARS 🔒 Security features
                                                            are included
                                                            Details on back.

PI-MATH BANK
   Mathematics USA

Memo _____   Signature _____   MP

⑆052341678⑆ 5125497653⑈ 2001

Name:.......................

Date: ....

Word Problems

1) While digging through his clothes for ice cream money, Mike found 8 quarters in his jacket, and 7 quarters in his shirt. How much money did Mike find?   _____

2) On Friday, Sara spent 9 pennies on ice cream. The next day, Sara spent 12 quarters on baseball cards. All in all, how much money did Sara spend?

_____

3) Sally got 12 quarters for washing clothes, and 6 nickels for house cleaning. How much money does Sally have?   _____

4) Keith found 14 quarters, 10 pennies, and 3 dimes in his house, and found 12 pennies in his piggybank. How much money did Keith find?

_____

5) Alyssa got 12 dimes and 10 quarters shining shoes, and in her tip jar found 8 quarters and 17 nickels. How much money did Alyssa get?   _____

6) When Tim was visited by the toothfairy, he received 6 each of pennies, dimes, and nickels. How much money did the toothfairy leave Tim?   _____

7) Mike sold lemonade in his neighborhood. He got 16 nickels on Saturday and 17 nickels on Sunday. What amount of money did Mike receive?   _____

8) On Saturday, Benny spent 4 pennies playing pinball. The next day, he spent 12 pennies on pinball. What was the total amount Benny spent playing pinball?

_____

9) Melanie has 16 quarters and 13 dimes. All in all, how much money does Melanie have?   _____

10) As Nancy was searching through her couch cushions, she found 3 nickels, and 8 dimes in the couch. How much money in total does Nancy have? _____

Name:.................................... **Date:** ....

Word Problems

1) Melanie got 6 pennies for mowing lawns, and 9 nickels for house cleaning. How much money does Melanie have? _____

2) Mary has 6 dimes and 17 pennies. All in all, how much money does Mary have? _____

3) On Wednesday, Sam spent 4 pennies playing pinball. The next day, he spent 8 pennies on pinball. What was the total amount Sam spent playing pinball?

_____

4) Joan sold lemonade in her neighborhood. She got 8 quarters on Saturday and 17 quarters on Sunday. What amount of money did Joan receive?

_____

5) Jason got 10 nickels and 6 quarters shining shoes, and in his tip jar found 2 quarters and 7 pennies. How much money did Jason get? _____

6) When Mike was visited by the toothfairy, he received 3 each of pennies, quarters, and dimes. How much money did the toothfairy leave Mike?

_____

7) As Tim was searching through his couch cushions, he found 13 pennies, and 10 nickels in the couch. How much money in total does Tim have?

_____

8) While digging through his clothes for ice cream money, Tim found 16 quarters in his shorts, and 10 quarters in his shirt. How much money did Tim find? _____

9) Dan found 18 dimes, 11 pennies, and 7 nickels in his house, and found 2 pennies in his piggybank. How much money did Dan find?

_____

10) On Friday, Sara spent 3 dimes on ice cream. The next day, Sara spent 6 nickels on baseball cards. All in all, how much money did Sara spend?

_____

1) When Mary was visited by the toothfairy, she received 9 each of pennies,
dimes, and quarters. How much money did the toothfairy leave Mary?

_____

2) While digging through her clothes for ice cream money, Jessica found 10
pennies in her shirt, and 18 pennies in her jacket. How much money
did Jessica find?

_____

3) As Joan was searching through her couch cushions, she found 15 nickels,
and 13 dimes in the couch. How much money in total does Joan have?

_____

4) Jason got 8 nickels for watering plants, and 6 quarters for
cleaning gutters. How much money does Jason have?

_____

5) Fred sold lemonade in his neighborhood. He got 7 dimes on Saturday
and 15 dimes on Sunday. What amount of money did Fred receive?

_____

6) Jason found 16 pennies, 11 nickels, and 9 dimes in his house,
and found 8 nickels in his piggybank. How much money did Jason find?

_____

7) On Friday, Jason spent 15 nickels on ice cream. The next day, Jason spent
2 pennies on baseball cards. All in all, how much money did Jason spend?

_____

8) On Tuesday, Melanie spent 13 quarters playing pinball. The next day, she spent
14 quarters on pinball. What was the total amount Melanie spent playing pinball?

_____

9) Alyssa got 13 nickels and 9 quarters shining shoes, and in her tip jar found
8 quarters and 3 pennies. How much money did Alyssa get?

_____

10) Sara has 8 nickels and 6 dimes. All in all, how much money does
Sara have?

_____

Word Problems

1) Tim sold lemonade in his neighborhood. He got seventeen nickels on Saturday and thirteen nickels on Sunday. What amount of money did Tim receive?

_____

2) As Jason was searching through his couch cushions, he found thirteen pennies, and fifteen nickels in the couch. How much money in total does Jason have?

_____

3) On Friday, Mike spent sixteen quarters on ice cream. The next day, Mike spent ten dimes on baseball cards. All in all, how much money did Mike spend?

_____

4) Fred got four pennies for house cleaning, and three nickels for watering plants. How much money does Fred have? _____

5) While digging through his clothes for ice cream money, Jason found ten quarters in his jacket, and fourteen quarters in his shirt. How much money did Jason find? _____

6) Sara has three dimes and twelve quarters. All in all, how much money does Sara have? _____

7) Tom found nine dimes, five quarters, and seven pennies in his house, and found two quarters in his piggybank. How much money did Tom find?

_____

8) On Sunday, Sam spent seventeen pennies playing pinball. The next day, he spent ten pennies on pinball. What was the total amount Sam spent playing pinball?

_____

9) Tim got three dimes and eight quarters shining shoes, and in his tip jar found ten quarters and fourteen pennies. How much money did Tim get?

_____

10) When Keith was visited by the toothfairy, he received seventeen each of pennies, nickels, and dimes. How much money did the toothfairy leave Keith?

_____

Word Problems

1) While digging through her clothes for ice cream money, Mary found sixteen pennies in her jacket, and seventeen pennies in her pants. How much money did Mary find? _____

2) Joan got five dimes and thirteen pennies shining shoes, and in her tip jar found fourteen pennies and twelve quarters. How much money did Joan get?

_____

3) Tim got seven dimes for mowing lawns, and sixteen pennies for house cleaning. How much money does Tim have? _____

4) Fred found eighteen quarters, three nickels, and seventeen dimes in his house, and found two nickels in his piggybank. How much money did Fred find?

_____

5) Jason sold lemonade in his neighborhood. He got thirteen quarters on Saturday and two quarters on Sunday. What amount of money did Jason receive?

_____

6) When Benny was visited by the toothfairy, he received seventeen each of nickels, quarters, and pennies. How much money did the toothfairy leave Benny?

_____

7) As Tim was searching through his couch cushions, he found three quarters, and seventeen pennies in the couch. How much money in total does Tim have?

_____

8) On Friday, Mike spent nine pennies playing pinball. The next day, he spent ten pennies on pinball. What was the total amount Mike spent playing pinball?

_____

9) Keith has twelve pennies and fourteen quarters. All in all, how much money does Keith have?

_____

10) On Friday, Mike spent eighteen pennies on ice cream. The next day, Mike spent seven quarters on baseball cards. All in all, how much money did Mike spend?

_____

Word Problems

1) Sandy sold lemonade in her neighborhood. She got eighteen pennies on Saturday and six pennies on Sunday. What amount of money did Sandy receive?

_____

2) Tim found sixteen dimes, two nickels, and three pennies in his house, and found ten nickels in his piggybank. How much money did Tim find?

_____

3) While digging through his clothes for ice cream money, Dan found nine pennies in his pants, and three pennies in his jacket. How much money did Dan find?

_____

4) Fred got ten dimes and fifteen quarters shining shoes, and in his tip jar found eighteen quarters and thirteen nickels. How much money did Fred get?

_____

5) As Jason was searching through his couch cushions, he found eight dimes, and fourteen nickels in the couch. How much money in total does Jason have?

_____

6) On Monday, Alyssa spent fifteen nickels playing pinball. The next day, she spent eight nickels on pinball. What was the total amount Alyssa spent playing pinball?

_____

7) When Sally was visited by the toothfairy, she received nine each of pennies, quarters, and dimes. How much money did the toothfairy leave Sally?

_____

8) Jason has nine quarters and three dimes. All in all, how much money does Jason have?

_____

9) On Friday, Mike spent seven pennies on ice cream. The next day, Mike spent seventeen dimes on baseball cards. All in all, how much money did Mike spend?

_____

10) Jason got three pennies for mowing lawns, and four dimes for watering plants. How much money does Jason have?   _____

Word Problems

1) Keith got fourteen quarters for washing clothes, and five pennies for
   washing dishes. How much money does Keith have? _____

2) On Monday, Mike spent sixteen pennies playing pinball. The next day, he spent
   ten pennies on pinball. What was the total amount Mike spent playing pinball?

   _____

3) On Friday, Sam spent 14 dimes on ice cream. The next day, Sam spent
   12 nickels on baseball cards. All in all, how much money did Sam spend?

   _____

4) As Sam was searching through his couch cushions, he found 2 nickels,
   and 16 quarters in the couch. How much money in total does Sam have?

   _____

5) Keith got 5 dimes and 8 nickels shining shoes, and in his tip jar found
   9 nickels and 16 pennies. How much money did Keith get? _____

6) Jessica has thirteen pennies and four nickels. All in all, how much money does
   Jessica have? _____

7) Nancy found five dimes, seven quarters, and thirteen nickels in her house,
   and found three quarters in her piggybank. How much money did Nancy find?

   _____

8) While digging through her clothes for ice cream money, Melanie found 6
   quarters in her shorts, and 16 quarters in her jacket. How much money
   did Melanie find? _____

9) When Benny was visited by the toothfairy, he received 9 each of pennies,
   quarters, and nickels. How much money did the toothfairy leave Benny?

   _____

10) Tom sold lemonade in his neighborhood. He got four quarters on Saturday
   and eleven quarters on Sunday. What amount of money did Tom receive?

   _____

1) As Benny was searching through his couch cushions, he found 18 dimes, and 5 quarters in the couch. How much money in total does Benny have?

_____

2) On Wednesday, Mike spent 10 dimes playing pinball. The next day, he spent 16 dimes on pinball. What was the total amount Mike spent playing pinball?

_____

3) Alyssa has eight pennies and eighteen nickels. All in all, how much money does Alyssa have?

_____

4) Sally got five quarters for mowing lawns, and sixteen nickels for cleaning gutters. How much money does Sally have?

_____

5) On Friday, Alyssa spent 9 quarters on ice cream. The next day, Alyssa spent 4 nickels on baseball cards. All in all, how much money did Alyssa spend?

_____

6) While digging through her clothes for ice cream money, Sally found four quarters in her shorts, and thirteen quarters in her pants. How much money did Sally find?

_____

7) When Joan was visited by the toothfairy, she received fifteen each of pennies, nickels, and quarters. How much money did the toothfairy leave Joan?

_____

8) Jessica got fourteen dimes and two nickels shining shoes, and in her tip jar found seventeen nickels and four quarters. How much money did Jessica get?

_____

9) Sara sold lemonade in her neighborhood. She got 13 nickels on Saturday and 4 nickels on Sunday. What amount of money did Sara receive?

_____

10) Jessica found 8 nickels, 5 quarters, and 14 pennies in her house, and found 3 quarters in her piggybank. How much money did Jessica find?

_____

Word Problems

1) When Joan was visited by the toothfairy, she received twelve each of nickels, quarters, and dimes. How much money did the toothfairy leave Joan?

_____

2) Mike sold lemonade in his neighborhood. He got 13 nickels on Saturday and 7 nickels on Sunday. What amount of money did Mike receive?

_____

3) On Tuesday, Dan spent 14 quarters playing pinball. The next day, he spent 12 quarters on pinball. What was the total amount Dan spent playing pinball?

_____

4) While digging through his clothes for ice cream money, Keith found 18 nickels in his shirt, and 5 nickels in his pants. How much money did Keith find?

_____

5) As Jason was searching through his couch cushions, he found six nickels, and seven quarters in the couch. How much money in total does Jason have?

_____

6) Sara found 7 nickels, 13 pennies, and 10 quarters in her house, and found 16 pennies in her piggybank. How much money did Sara find?

_____

7) Jessica got sixteen quarters for mowing lawns, and seventeen pennies for washing dishes. How much money does Jessica have?

_____

8) Sandy has 12 pennies and 5 nickels. All in all, how much money does Sandy have?

_____

9) On Friday, Jason spent thirteen pennies on ice cream. The next day, Jason spent ten dimes on baseball cards. All in all, how much money did Jason spend?

_____

10) Alyssa got four dimes and eighteen pennies shining shoes, and in her tip jar found fourteen pennies and fifteen nickels. How much money did Alyssa get?

_____

Word Problems

1) On Monday, Mary spent 3 pennies playing pinball. The next day, she spent
6 pennies on pinball. What was the total amount Mary spent playing pinball?

_____

2) Sam has eighteen quarters and seventeen nickels. All in all, how much money does
Sam have?

_____

3) Dan found 3 pennies, 15 quarters, and 5 dimes in his house,
and found 10 quarters in his piggybank. How much money did Dan find?

_____

4) Melanie got 6 pennies for washing dishes, and 2 quarters for
watering plants. How much money does Melanie have?   _____

5) Alyssa sold lemonade in her neighborhood. She got 16 dimes on Saturday
and 15 dimes on Sunday. What amount of money did Alyssa receive?

_____

6) While digging through his clothes for ice cream money, Dan found thirteen
pennies in his shorts, and ten pennies in his pants. How much money
did Dan find?   _____

7) As Mary was searching through her couch cushions, she found six nickels,
and two pennies in the couch. How much money in total does Mary have?

_____

8) Joan got nine quarters and eleven nickels shining shoes, and in her tip jar found
five nickels and sixteen dimes. How much money did Joan get?   _____

9) When Benny was visited by the toothfairy, he received 8 each of quarters,
nickels, and pennies. How much money did the toothfairy leave Benny?

_____

10) On Friday, Keith spent eighteen quarters on ice cream. The next day, Keith spent
fifteen pennies on baseball cards. All in all, how much money did Keith spend?

_____

Name:.................................

Date: ....

Word Problems

1) Joan spent $14.12 on a gerbil toy, and a cage cost her $12.13. What was the total cost of Joan's purchases? _____

2) Benny joined his school's band. He bought a trombone for $137.62, and a song book which was $14.32. How much did Benny spend at the music store? _____

3) Benny purchased a Pokemon game for $6.53, and a Spiderman game for $8.09. How much did Benny spend on video games? _____

4) On Saturday, Dan spent $8.04 each on two tickets to a movie theater. He also borrowed a movie for $14.86. How much money in total did Dan spend on movies?

_____

5) Alyssa bought some toys. She bought a football for $9.62, and spent $4.51 on marbles. In total, how much did Alyssa spend on toys? _____

6) Mary loves eating fruits. Mary paid $12.30 for apples, and $9.89 for grapes. In total, how much money did Mary spend? _____

7) Tom loves trading cards. She bought 3 packs of baseball cards for $2.56 each, and a deck of Pokemon cards for $12.52. How much did Tom spend on cards?

_____

8) For her car, Sara spent $111.12 on speakers and $117.28 on new tires. In total, how much did Sara spend on car parts? _____

9) Sam went to the mall on Saturday to buy clothes. He spent $10.86 on shorts and $9.08 on pants. In total, how much money did Sam spend on clothing? _____

10) Dan got fast food for lunch. Dan spent $5.06 on a hotdog and $5.31 on fries. What was the total of the lunch bill? _____

Word Problems

1) Jessica purchased a Batman game for $4.53, and a Spiderman game for $13.58. How much did Jessica spend on video games? _____

2) Nancy spent $10.28 on a rabbit toy, and a cage cost her $12.49. What was the total cost of Nancy's purchases? _____

3) Benny went to the mall on Saturday to buy clothes. He spent $8.55 on a shirt and $12.67 on pants. In total, how much money did Benny spend on clothing? _____

4) Mary bought some toys. She bought a skateboard for $12.79, and spent $9.92 on a football. In total, how much did Mary spend on toys? _____

5) Joan loves eating fruits. Joan paid $9.01 for grapes, and $4.60 for cherries. In total, how much money did Joan spend? _____

6) For her car, Nancy spent $127.93 on speakers and $143.42 on new tires. In total, how much did Nancy spend on car parts? _____

7) Joan loves trading cards. She bought 3 packs of football cards for $2.17 each, and a deck of Digimon cards for $12.43. How much did Joan spend on cards?

_____

8) On Tuesday, Sam spent $9.50 each on two tickets to a movie theater. He also borrowed a movie for $14.18. How much money in total did Sam spend on movies?

_____

9) Joan got fast food for lunch. Joan spent $3.57 on a sandwich and $2.95 on a salad. What was the total of the lunch bill? _____

10) Fred joined his school's band. He bought a flute for $119.49, and a song book which was $11.73. How much did Fred spend at the music store? _____

Word Problems

1) Fred spent $9.78 on a cat toy, and a cage cost him $8.88. What was the total cost of Fred's purchases?

   _____

2) Alyssa loves eating fruits. Alyssa paid $13.77 for bananas, and $14.43 for grapes. In total, how much money did Alyssa spend?

   _____

3) For his car, Dan spent $102.47 on speakers and $121.84 on new tires. In total, how much did Dan spend on car parts?

   _____

4) Dan bought some toys. He bought a football for $4.25, and spent $12.88 on toy cars. In total, how much did Dan spend on toys?

   _____

5) Keith joined his school's band. He bought a violin for $135.98, and a song book which was $11.54. How much did Keith spend at the music store?

   _____

6) Melanie went to the mall on Saturday to buy clothes. She spent $7.94 on pants and $13.26 on shorts. In total, how much money did Melanie spend on clothing?

   _____

7) On Wednesday, Sara spent $10.30 each on two tickets to a movie theater. She also borrowed a movie for $13.93. How much money in total did Sara spend on movies?

   _____

8) Dan purchased a racing game for $11.11, and a Superman game for $9.71. How much did Dan spend on video games?

   _____

9) Sally got fast food for lunch. Sally spent $3.31 on a sandwich and $2.16 on soup. What was the total of the lunch bill?

   _____

10) Dan loves trading cards. She bought 3 packs of football cards for $4.08 each, and a deck of baseball cards for $14.83. How much did Dan spend on cards?

   _____

Name: .... **Date:** ....

Word Problems

1) Joan purchased a Spiderman game for $14.58, and a basketball game for $14.96. How much did Joan spend on video games? _____

2) Tom loves eating fruits. Tom paid $5.02 for grapes, and $8.78 for bananas. In total, how much money did Tom spend? _____

3) Keith went to the mall on Saturday to buy clothes. He spent $12 on pants and $4.77 on a shirt. In total, how much money did Keith spend on clothing?

_____

4) On Saturday, Melanie spent $9.83 each on two tickets to a movie theater. She also borrowed a movie for $9.41. How much money in total did Melanie spend on movies?

_____

5) Keith joined his school's band. He bought a trombone for $146.24, and a song book which was $8.56. How much did Keith spend at the music store? _____

6) Sam bought some toys. He bought marbles for $11.83, and spent $14.19 on toy cars. In total, how much did Sam spend on toys? _____

7) For his car, Dan spent $134.22 on speakers and $103.80 on new tires. In total, how much did Dan spend on car parts? _____

8) Nancy loves trading cards. He bought 3 packs of football cards for $3.71 each, and a deck of Digimon cards for $7.77. How much did Nancy spend on cards?

_____

9) Alyssa got fast food for lunch. Alyssa spent $4.27 on soup and $3.64 on a hamburger. What was the total of the lunch bill? _____

10) Mary spent $10.97 on a lizard toy, and a cage cost her $9.54. What was the total cost of Mary's purchases? _____

Name:................................. **Date:** ....

Word Problems

1) Alyssa bought some toys. She bought a baseball for $11.27, and spent $8.09 on toy trucks. In total, how much did Alyssa spend on toys?

_____

2) Tom loves eating fruits. Tom paid $8.61 for cherries, and $9.90 for grapes. In total, how much money did Tom spend?

_____

3) Jason spent $5.03 on a lizard toy, and a cage cost him $4.61. What was the total cost of Jason's purchases?

_____

4) Sally purchased a Batman game for $13.98, and a baseball game for $13.39. How much did Sally spend on video games?

_____

5) Nancy went to the mall on Saturday to buy clothes. She spent $14.12 on pants and $10.20 on shorts. In total, how much money did Nancy spend on clothing?

_____

6) On Monday, Tom spent $9.91 each on two tickets to a movie theater. He also borrowed a movie for $10.64. How much money in total did Tom spend on movies?

_____

7) Melanie got fast food for lunch. Melanie spent $4.39 on a sandwich and $4.12 on a shake. What was the total of the lunch bill?

_____

8) Mike joined his school's band. He bought a guitar for $104.40, and a song book which was $13.73. How much did Mike spend at the music store?

_____

9) Melanie loves trading cards. He bought 4 packs of baseball cards for $4.28 each, and a deck of Pokemon cards for $12.30. How much did Melanie spend on cards?

_____

10) For his car, Keith spent $126.65 on speakers and $120.27 on new tires. In total, how much did Keith spend on car parts?

_____

Word Problems

1) Fred loves eating fruits. Fred paid $4.28 for grapes, $8.91 for cherries, and $7.01 for peaches. In total, how much money did he spend? _____

2) Sam went to the mall to buy clothes. He spent $8.65 on pants, $13.76 on a shirt, and $12.56 on shorts. How much money did Sam spend on clothes? _____

3) Joan joined her school's band. She bought a viola for $136.72, a music stand for $6.79, and a song book for $4.28. How much did Joan spend at the music store? _____

4) Jessica purchased a Pokemon game for $14.61, a strategy game for $6.89, and a baseball game for $7.69. How much did Jessica spend on video games? _____

5) Nancy loves trading cards. She bought 2 packs of football cards for $4.88 each, a pack of Digimon cards for $1.65, and a deck of basketball cards for $8.19. How much did Nancy spend on cards? _____

6) Benny got fast food for lunch. He spent $4.02 on soup, $1.12 on a hotdog, and $1 on a salad. What was the total of the lunch bill? _____

7) Melanie spent $7.21 on a dog toy, $3.30 on pet food, and a cage cost her $14.59. What was the total cost of Melanie's purchases? _____

8) Dan spent $103.52 on speakers, $138.07 on a CD player, and $132.20 on new tires. In total, how much did Dan spend on car parts? _____

9) On Saturday, Tim spent $5.36 each on two tickets to a movie theater. He also rented a movie for $5.23, and bought a movie for $4.04. How much money in total did Tim spend on movies? _____

10) Jason bought some toys. He bought a football for $6.90, toy cars for $14.43, and spent $4.62 on toy trucks. In total, how much did Jason spend on toys? _____

Word Problems

1) Sandy loves eating fruits. Sandy paid $6.54 for bananas, $10.61 for berries, and $10.25 for grapes. In total, how much money did she spend? _____

2) Melanie went to the mall to buy clothes. She spent $8.56 on pants, $5.33 on a shirt, and $8.34 on a jacket. How much money did Melanie spend on clothes?

_____

3) Nancy joined her school's band. She bought a flute for $102.77, a music stand for $13.91, and a song book for $7.44. How much did Nancy spend at the music store?

_____

4) Alyssa purchased a Batman game for $8.27, a strategy game for $13.92, and a racing game for $4.89. How much did Alyssa spend on video games?

_____

5) Fred loves trading cards. She bought 2 packs of Pokemon cards for $3.19 each, a pack of baseball cards for $2.28, and a deck of football cards for $5.26. How much did Fred spend on cards? _____

6) Mike got fast food for lunch. He spent $4.79 on a hotdog, $2.70 on fries, and $1.89 on a hamburger. What was the total of the lunch bill? _____

7) Nancy spent $14.92 on a lizard toy, $4.24 on pet food, and a cage cost her $11.07. What was the total cost of Nancy's purchases? _____

8) Nancy spent $145.20 on speakers, $130.83 on a CD player, and $118 on new tires. In total, how much did Nancy spend on car parts? _____

9) On Thursday, Benny spent $8.03 each on two tickets to a movie theater. He also rented a movie for $1.93, and bought a movie for $10.26. How much money in total did Benny spend on movies? _____

10) Mary bought some toys. She bought toy trucks for $8.22, a skateboard for $11.40, and spent $14.27 on marbles. In total, how much did Mary spend on toys?

_____

Word Problems

1) Sara loves eating fruits. Sara paid $7.62 for berries, $6.75 for peaches, and $4.52 for bananas. In total, how much money did she spend? _____

2) Tom went to the mall to buy clothes. He spent $5.08 on a shirt, $10 on a jacket, and $5.75 on pants. How much money did Tom spend on clothes?

_____

3) Sam joined his school's band. He bought a cello for $145.12, a music stand for $9.42, and a song book for $10.67. How much did Sam spend at the music store?

_____

4) Nancy purchased a football game for $9.84, a strategy game for $13.75, and a baseball game for $12.06. How much did Nancy spend on video games?

_____

5) Mary loves trading cards. He bought 2 packs of Digimon cards for $4.91 each, a pack of basketball cards for $2.64, and a deck of football cards for $11.32. How much did Mary spend on cards? _____

6) Nancy got fast food for lunch. She spent $1.27 on a sandwich, $3.99 on soup, and $3.04 on a salad. What was the total of the lunch bill? _____

7) Sandy spent $10.81 on a dog toy, $2.28 on pet food, and a cage cost her $5.10. What was the total cost of Sandy's purchases? _____

8) Mary spent $144.51 on speakers, $149.82 on a CD player, and $111.47 on new tires. In total, how much did Mary spend on car parts? _____

9) On Monday, Keith spent $9.23 each on two tickets to a movie theater. He also rented a movie for $1.44, and bought a movie for $10.78. How much money in total did Keith spend on movies? _____

10) Fred bought some toys. He bought a baseball for $9.43, a football for $5.57, and spent $11.06 on a skateboard. In total, how much did Fred spend on toys?

_____

Word Problems

1) Mary loves eating fruits. Mary paid $8.50 for apples, $6.59 for peaches, and
   $9.99 for bananas. In total, how much money did she spend?   _____

2) Joan went to the mall to buy clothes. She spent $8.45 on shorts, $12.26 on pants,
   and $4.33 on a shirt. How much money did Joan spend on clothes?

   _____

3) Jason joined his school's band. He bought a violin for $108.99, a music stand for
   $8.80, and a song book for $8.97. How much did Jason spend at the music store?

   _____

4) Sam purchased a baseball game for $11.25, a strategy game for $10.73, and a
   Pokemon game for $7.10. How much did Sam spend on video games?

   _____

5) Melanie loves trading cards. He bought 2 packs of Digimon cards for $1.81 each, a
   pack of baseball cards for $4.10, and a deck of Pokemon cards for $7.08. How
   much did Melanie spend on cards?   _____

6) Dan got fast food for lunch. He spent $4.24 on a sandwich, $4.80 on a hamburger,
   and $3.22 on a salad. What was the total of the lunch bill?   _____

7) Melanie spent $5.39 on a dog toy, $4.83 on pet food, and a cage cost her $12.16.
   What was the total cost of Melanie's purchases?   _____

8) Sally spent $114.36 on speakers, $148.77 on a CD player, and $121.93 on new
   tires. In total, how much did Sally spend on car parts?   _____

9) On Friday, Sandy spent $5.30 each on two tickets to a movie theater. She also
   rented a movie for $2.48, and bought a movie for $5.84. How much money in total
   did Sandy spend on movies?   _____

10) Sandy bought some toys. She bought a skateboard for $5.45, toy cars for $6.96,
    and spent $6.05 on a football. In total, how much did Sandy spend on toys?

    _____

Name:..   **Date:** ....

Word Problems

1) Mike loves eating fruits. Mike paid $9.83 for peaches, $13.31 for berries, and $15 for cherries. In total, how much money did he spend?   _____

2) Sam went to the mall to buy clothes. He spent $11.77 on a shirt, $9.78 on shorts, and $13.85 on a jacket. How much money did Sam spend on clothes?

    _____

3) Sara joined her school's band. She bought a guitar for $132.81, a music stand for $14.05, and a song book for $8.30. How much did Sara spend at the music store?

    _____

4) Nancy purchased a football game for $9.62, a strategy game for $13.94, and a racing game for $5.55. How much did Nancy spend on video games?

    _____

5) Nancy loves trading cards. She bought 2 packs of basketball cards for $2.93 each, a pack of football cards for $5, and a deck of Pokemon cards for $11.68. How much did Nancy spend on cards?   _____

6) Mary got fast food for lunch. She spent $3.22 on a salad, $5.09 on a hotdog, and $4.39 on fries. What was the total of the lunch bill?   _____

7) Keith spent $6.83 on a lizard toy, $3.79 on pet food, and a cage cost him $14.68. What was the total cost of Keith's purchases?   _____

8) Joan spent $149.26 on speakers, $149.14 on a CD player, and $134.98 on new tires. In total, how much did Joan spend on car parts?   _____

9) On Sunday, Nancy spent $14.25 each on two tickets to a movie theater. She also rented a movie for $3.28, and bought a movie for $9.87. How much money in total did Nancy spend on movies?   _____

10) Sam bought some toys. He bought a skateboard for $14.53, toy trucks for $4.18, and spent $8.06 on toy cars. In total, how much did Sam spend on toys?

    _____

Word Problems

1) Keith loves eating fruits. Keith paid $9.53 for grapes, and $14.89 for apples with two $20 bills. How much change did Keith receive?   _____

2) Sandy went to the mall on Saturday to buy clothes. She paid $5.94 on a shirt and $13.63 on a jacket with a $20 bill. How much money did Sandy get in change?

_____

3) Mary joined her school's band. She bought a viola for $88.47, and a song book which was $4.78 with a $100 bill. How much change was Mary given?   _____

4) Tim purchased a baseball game for $5.65, and a football game for $11.30 with a $20 bill. How much change did Tim get?

5) Jessica loves trading cards. She bought 4 packs of Digimon cards for $2.58 each, and a deck of basketball cards for $9.63 with a $20 bill. How much change did Jessica get?

_____

6) Jason got fast food for lunch. Jason paid $2.68 on a hotdog and $1.57 on a shake with a $10 bill. What was the change from the purchase?   _____

7) Sandy paid $9.45 on a lizard toy, and a cage cost her $5.58 with a $20 bill. How much change did Sandy receive?   _____

8) For his car, Jason paid $97.72 on speakers and $91.65 on new tires with two $100 bills. How much did Jason get in change?   _____

9) On Monday, Benny paid $4.20 each on two tickets to a movie theater. He also borrowed a movie for $11.66. Benny paid with two $20 bills. How much change did Benny receive?   _____

10) Jason bought some toys. He bought a baseball for $4.64, and paid $11.60 on toy trucks with a $20 bill. How much change from the purchase?   _____

Word Problems

1) Sam loves eating fruits. Sam paid $5.41 for bananas, and $5.70 for apples with a $20 bill. How much change did Sam receive? _____

2) Sandy went to the mall on Saturday to buy clothes. She paid $8.27 on shorts and $9.31 on a shirt with a $20 bill. How much money did Sandy get in change?

_____

3) Jessica joined her school's band. She bought a trombone for $86.41, and a song book which was $11.72 with a $100 bill. How much change was Jessica given?

_____

4) Sandy purchased a racing game for $13.75, and a baseball game for $5.11 with a $20 bill. How much change did Sandy get? _____

5) Jessica loves trading cards. She bought 4 packs of Pokemon cards for $1.29 each, and a deck of football cards for $6.12 with a $20 bill. How much change did Jessica get?

_____

6) Alyssa got fast food for lunch. Alyssa paid $2.44 on a hamburger and $5.88 on a shake with a $10 bill. What was the change from the purchase? _____

7) Mike paid $4.18 on a dog toy, and a cage cost him $8.83 with a $20 bill. How much change did Mike receive? _____

8) For his car, Fred paid $91.23 on speakers and $95.07 on new tires with two $100 bills. How much did Fred get in change? _____

9) On Tuesday, Jessica paid $13.91 each on two tickets to a movie theater. She also borrowed a movie for $8.81. Jessica paid with two $20 bills. How much change did Jessica receive? _____

10) Alyssa bought some toys. She bought toy cars for $6.77, and paid $7.03 on toy trucks with a $20 bill. How much change from the purchase? _____

Word Problems

1) Jessica loves eating fruits. Jessica paid $8.60 for cherries, and $8.10 for berries with a $20 bill. How much change did Jessica receive? _____

2) Jason went to the mall on Saturday to buy clothes. He paid $4.13 on a shirt and $10.69 on shorts with a $20 bill. How much money did Jason get in change? _____

3) Jason joined his school's band. He bought a viola for $86.56, and a song book which was $8.61 with a $100 bill. How much change was Jason given? _____

4) Sandy purchased a Pokemon game for $13.86, and a football game for $6.22 with two $20 bills. How much change did Sandy get? _____

5) Jason loves trading cards. He bought 2 packs of baseball cards for $4.07 each, and a deck of Pokemon cards for $14.97 with two $20 bills. How much change did Jason get? _____

6) Benny got fast food for lunch. Benny paid $4.06 on a hotdog and $4.98 on a salad with a $10 bill. What was the change from the purchase? _____

7) Benny paid $7.20 on a dog toy, and a cage cost him $4.67 with a $20 bill. How much change did Benny receive? _____

8) For his car, Tom paid $89.76 on speakers and $92.72 on new tires with two $100 bills. How much did Tom get in change? _____

9) On Thursday, Joan paid $10.95 each on two tickets to a movie theater. She also borrowed a movie for $13.03. Joan paid with two $20 bills. How much change did Joan receive? _____

10) Jessica bought some toys. She bought marbles for $6.39, and paid $6.71 on toy cars with a $20 bill. How much change from the purchase? _____

Word Problems

1) Mike loves eating fruits. Mike paid $8.99 for grapes, and $4.90 for berries with a $20 bill. How much change did Mike receive? _____

2) Mike went to the mall on Saturday to buy clothes. He paid $7.63 on shorts and $6.10 on pants with a $20 bill. How much money did Mike get in change? _____

3) Mike joined his school's band. He bought a flute for $84.08, and a song book which was $10.91 with a $100 bill. How much change was Mike given? _____

4) Dan purchased a baseball game for $6.80, and a racing game for $13.24 with two $20 bills. How much change did Dan get? _____

5) Melanie loves trading cards. She bought 4 packs of basketball cards for $3.36 each, and a deck of Pokemon cards for $7.73 with two $20 bills. How much change did Melanie get? _____

6) Dan got fast food for lunch. Dan paid $5.89 on a salad and $1.07 on a sandwich with a $10 bill. What was the change from the purchase? _____

7) Mary paid $10.39 on a lizard toy, and a cage cost her $10.34 with two $20 bills. How much change did Mary receive? _____

8) For her car, Alyssa paid $92.09 on speakers and $76.43 on new tires with two $100 bills. How much did Alyssa get in change? _____

9) On Thursday, Melanie paid $5.67 each on two tickets to a movie theater. She also borrowed a movie for $7.37. Melanie paid with a $20 bill. How much change did Melanie receive? _____

10) Dan bought some toys. He bought a baseball for $10.74, and paid $10.90 on a football with two $20 bills. How much change from the purchase? _____

Word Problems

1) Jason loves eating fruits. Jason paid $14.57 for apples, and $11.53 for cherries with two $20 bills. How much change did Jason receive? _____

2) Mike went to the mall on Saturday to buy clothes. He paid $12.84 on pants and $13.80 on shorts with two $20 bills. How much money did Mike get in change?

_____

3) Mike joined his school's band. He bought a flute for $72.91, and a song book which was $13.80 with a $100 bill. How much change was Mike given? _____

4) Sam purchased a Superman game for $4.56, and a football game for $12.90 with a $20 bill. How much change did Sam get? _____

5) Dan loves trading cards. He bought 3 packs of Digimon cards for $3.45 each, and a deck of baseball cards for $8.63 with a $20 bill. How much change did Dan get?

_____

6) Alyssa got fast food for lunch. Alyssa paid $5.27 on a hotdog and $4.74 on a hamburger with two $10 bills. What was the change from the purchase?

_____

7) Sandy paid $10.47 on a dog toy, and a cage cost her $8.16 with a $20 bill. How much change did Sandy receive? _____

8) For his car, Benny paid $98.78 on speakers and $85.80 on new tires with two $100 bills. How much did Benny get in change? _____

9) On Thursday, Mary paid $7.79 each on two tickets to a movie theater. She also borrowed a movie for $5.71. Mary paid with two $20 bills. How much change did Mary receive? _____

10) Benny bought some toys. He bought toy trucks for $7.70, and paid $10.85 on marbles with a $20 bill. How much change from the purchase? _____

Name: ....   Date: ....

Word Problems

1) Alyssa loves eating fruits. Alyssa paid $14.19 for grapes, and $14.17 for berries with two
   $20 bills. How much change did Alyssa receive?   _____

2) Dan went to the mall on Saturday to buy clothes. He paid $8.57 on shorts and
   $8.25 on a shirt with a $20 bill. How much money did Dan get in change?

   _____

3) Nancy joined her school's band. She bought a flute for $71.45, and a song book
   which was $8.23 with a $100 bill. How much change was Nancy given? _____

4) Dan purchased a Batman game for $12.37, and a Superman game for $10.25
   with two $20 bills. How much change did Dan get?   _____

5) Nancy loves trading cards. She bought 3 packs of football cards for $4.91 each, and
   a deck of basketball cards for $8.37 with two $20 bills. How much change did Nancy get?

   _____

6) Nancy got fast food for lunch. Nancy paid $2.53 on a shake and $5.72 on
   a hotdog with a $10 bill. What was the change from the purchase?   _____

7) Mike paid $14.81 on a gerbil toy, and a cage cost him $5.45 with two $20 bills.
   How much change did Mike receive?   _____

8) For his car, Dan paid $88.81 on speakers and $99.34 on new tires with
   two $100 bills. How much did Dan get in change?   _____

9) On Saturday, Tom paid $10.58 each on two tickets to a movie theater. He also borrowed
   a movie for $13.48. Tom paid with two $20 bills. How much change
   did Tom receive?   _____

10) Mike bought some toys. He bought marbles for $8.34, and paid $8.98
    on a baseball with a $20 bill. How much change from the purchase?   _____

Word Problems

1) Mike loves eating fruits. Mike paid $4.71 for berries, and $9.45 for bananas with a $20 bill. How much change did Mike receive? _____

2) Fred went to the mall on Saturday to buy clothes. He paid $5.74 on a jacket and $5.66 on shorts with a $20 bill. How much money did Fred get in change? _____

3) Sam joined his school's band. He bought a guitar for $76.01, and a song book which was $6.83 with a $100 bill. How much change was Sam given? _____

4) Sam purchased a football game for $5.58, and a Superman game for $13.94 with a $20 bill. How much change did Sam get? _____

5) Dan loves trading cards. He bought 3 packs of basketball cards for $4.47 each, and a deck of Pokemon cards for $7.78 with two $20 bills. How much change did Dan get? _____

6) Fred got fast food for lunch. Fred paid $1.88 on a sandwich and $3.86 on a salad with a $10 bill. What was the change from the purchase? _____

7) Sandy paid $6.23 on a cat toy, and a cage cost her $7.54 with a $20 bill. How much change did Sandy receive? _____

8) For his car, Fred paid $86.21 on speakers and $75.31 on new tires with two $100 bills. How much did Fred get in change? _____

9) On Sunday, Melanie paid $5.99 each on two tickets to a movie theater. She also borrowed a movie for $6.56. Melanie paid with a $20 bill. How much change did Melanie receive? _____

10) Dan bought some toys. He bought a baseball for $5.54, and paid $7.51 on toy trucks with a $20 bill. How much change from the purchase? _____

Word Problems

1) Mary loves eating fruits. Mary paid $5.02 for cherries, and $11.77 for apples with a $20 bill. How much change did Mary receive? _____

2) Nancy went to the mall on Saturday to buy clothes. She paid $8.70 on pants and $14.79 on a shirt with two $20 bills. How much money did Nancy get in change?

   _____

3) Nancy joined her school's band. She bought a trumpet for $99.09, and a song book which was $14.09 with two $100 bills. How much change was Nancy given? _____

4) Jessica purchased a Batman game for $12.12, and a racing game for $10.73 with two $20 bills. How much change did Jessica get? _____

5) Jessica loves trading cards. She bought 4 packs of basketball cards for $4.52 each, and a deck of Pokemon cards for $8.34 with two $20 bills. How much change did Jessica get?

   _____

6) Jessica got fast food for lunch. Jessica paid $2.53 on a salad and $4.51 on a sandwich with a $10 bill. What was the change from the purchase? _____

7) Jason paid $12.69 on a snake toy, and a cage cost him $6.90 with a $20 bill. How much change did Jason receive? _____

8) For his car, Sam paid $90.20 on speakers and $70.09 on new tires with two $100 bills. How much did Sam get in change? _____

9) On Wednesday, Mike paid $4.04 each on two tickets to a movie theater. He also borrowed a movie for $5.55. Mike paid with a $20 bill. How much change did Mike receive? _____

10) Jessica bought some toys. She bought a football for $5.82, and paid $4.31 on toy trucks with a $20 bill. How much change from the purchase? _____

Word Problems

1) Sandy loves eating fruits. Sandy paid $10.22 for berries, and $6.17 for peaches with a $20 bill. How much change did Sandy receive? _____

2) Mary went to the mall on Saturday to buy clothes. She paid $5.61 on shorts and $5.96 on pants with a $20 bill. How much money did Mary get in change?

_____

3) Dan joined his school's band. He bought a trombone for $97.97, and a song book which was $10.77 with two $100 bills. How much change was Dan given?_____

4) Jason purchased a racing game for $12.60, and a basketball game for $14.02 with two $20 bills. How much change did Jason get? _____

5) Melanie loves trading cards. She bought 4 packs of football cards for $2.17 each, and a deck of Pokemon cards for $13.49 with two $20 bills. How much change did Melanie get?

_____

6) Alyssa got fast food for lunch. Alyssa paid $5.13 on a hotdog and $4.21 on a salad with a $10 bill. What was the change from the purchase? _____

7) Joan paid $11.22 on a rabbit toy, and a cage cost her $11.93 with two $20 bills. How much change did Joan receive? _____

8) For his car, Jason paid $99.63 on speakers and $89.70 on new tires with two $100 bills. How much did Jason get in change? _____

9) On Tuesday, Tim paid $8.65 each on two tickets to a movie theater. He also borrowed a movie for $11.67. Tim paid with two $20 bills. How much change did Tim receive? _____

10) Mary bought some toys. She bought marbles for $11.86, and paid $10.02 on a football with two $20 bills. How much change from the purchase? _____

Word Problems

1) Alyssa loves eating fruits. Alyssa paid $9.16 for grapes, and $13.96 for apples with two $20 bills. How much change did Alyssa receive? _____

2) Dan went to the mall on Saturday to buy clothes. He paid $6.16 on a shirt and $8.27 on pants with a $20 bill. How much money did Dan get in change?

_____

3) Tim joined his school's band. He bought a violin for $88.94, and a song book which was $14.40 with two $100 bills. How much change was Tim given?

_____

4) Alyssa purchased a Superman game for $4.95, and a baseball game for $14.83 with a $20 bill. How much change did Alyssa get? _____

5) Alyssa loves trading cards. She bought 4 packs of basketball cards for $2.92 each, and a deck of Pokemon cards for $4.45 with a $20 bill. How much change did Alyssa get?

_____

6) Benny got fast food for lunch. Benny paid $1.77 on fries and $4 on a hotdog with a $10 bill. What was the change from the purchase? _____

7) Dan paid $6.29 on a dog toy, and a cage cost him $9.94 with a $20 bill. How much change did Dan receive? _____

8) For her car, Sara paid $79.40 on speakers and $84.78 on new tires with two $100 bills. How much did Sara get in change? _____

9) On Wednesday, Sara paid $4.45 each on two tickets to a movie theater. She also borrowed a movie for $8.96. Sara paid with a $20 bill. How much change did Sara receive? _____

10) Sam bought some toys. He bought toy cars for $10.26, and paid $10.27 on a skateboard with two $20 bills. How much change from the purchase?

_____

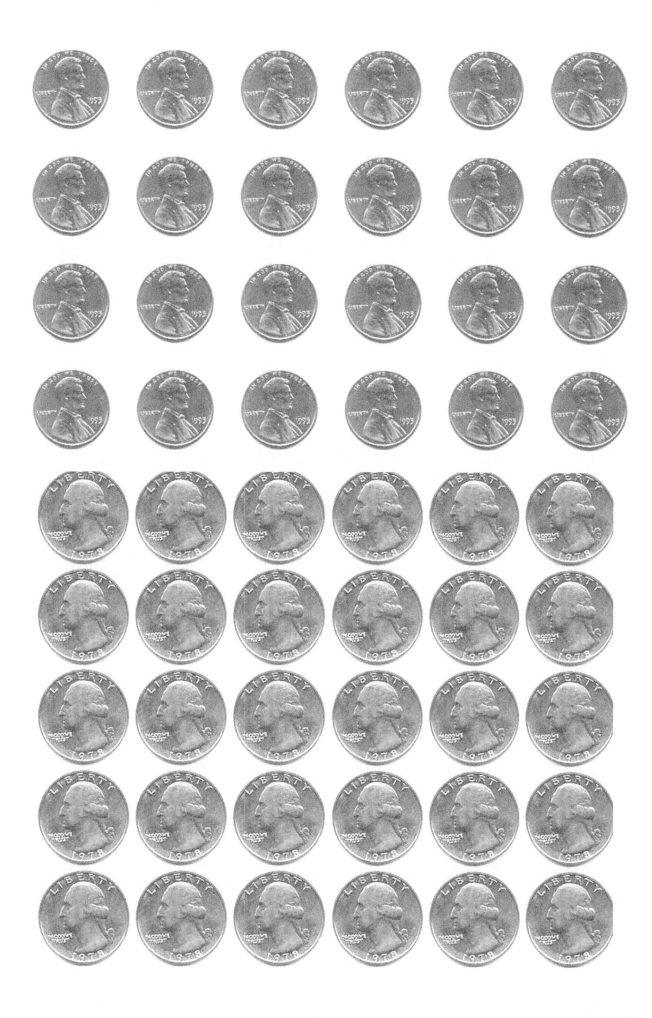

ANSWER KEY

DAY 1
1) $ 1.02
2) $ 1.56
3) $ 1.16
4) $ 1.57
5) $ 1.71
6) $ 1.57
7) $ 1.71
8) $ 1.67
9) $ 1.71

DAY 2
1) $ 24
2) $ 18
3) $ 30
4) $ 24
5) $ 35
6) $ 26
7) $ 30
8) $ 18

DAY 3
1) $ 0.96
2) $ 1.67
3) $ 1.67
4) $ 1.22
5) $ 1.01
6) $ 1.71
7) $ 1.21
8) $ 1.56
9) $ 1.08

DAY 4
1) $ 29
2) $ 18
3) $ 24
4) $ 26
5) $ 23
6) $ 33
7) $ 22
8) $ 18

DAY 5
1) $ 1.63
2) $ 2.21
3) $ 1.07
4) $ 2.21
5) $ 1.11
6) $ 1.93
7) $ 1.74

DAY 6
1) $ 37
2) $ 37
3) $ 40
4) $ 45
5) $ 18

DAY 7
1) $ 1.02
2) $ 2.37
3) $ 2.01
4) $ 2.62
5) $ 2.56
6) $ 1.88

DAY 8
1) $ 43
2) $ 33
3) $ 41
4) $ 50
5) $ 18

DAY 9
1) $ 2.82
2) $ 1.73
3) $ 1.64
4) $ 1.41
5) $ 2.04
6) $ 1.66

DAY 10
1) $ 57
2) $ 39
3) $ 67
4) $ 44
5) $ 36

DAY 11
1) $ 1.93
2) $ 3.06
3) $ 1.62
4) $ 2.01
5) $ 1.71
6) $ 1.16

DAY 12
1) $ 57
2) $ 38
3) $ 36
4) $ 34
5) $ 18

DAY 13
1) $ 4.10
2) $ 3.98
3) $ 2.40
4) $ 1.24
5) $ 1.22
6) $ 1.39

DAY 14
1) $ 430
2) $ 430
3) $ 340
4) $ 390
5) $ 520
6) $ 300
7) $ 180

DAY 15
1) $ 3.08
2) $ 2.31
3) $ 1.73
4) $ 2.99
5) $ 2.20
6) $ 1.22

DAY 16
1) $ 460
2) $ 380
3) $ 400
4) $ 320
5) $ 440
6) $ 180

DAY 17
1) $ 2.17
2) $ 3.19
3) $ 3.86
4) $ 2.67
5) $ 2.36
6) $ 1.81

DAY 18
1) $ 680
2) $ 690
3) $ 680
4) $ 220
5) $ 340
6) $ 180

DAY 19
1) $ 4.49
2) $ 4.46
3) $ 2.96
4) $ 2.89
5) $ 1.79

DAY 20
1) $ 480
2) $ 520
3) $ 540
4) $ 390
5) $ 360

DAY 21
1) $ 18.41
2) $ 18.41
3) $ 18.41
4) $ 18.41
5) $ 18.41
6) $ 18.41
7) $ 35.11

DAY 22
1) $ 18.41
2) $ 18.41
3) $ 18.41
4) $ 18.41
5) $ 18.41
6) $ 18.41
7) $ 24.91

DAY 23
1) $ 36.46
2) $ 31.47
3) $ 18.66
4) $ 36.72
5) $ 18.53

DAY 24
1) $ 25.57
2) $ 23.76
3) $ 33.82
4) $ 18.51
5) $ 20.82

DAY 25
1) $ 25.51
2) $ 42.87
3) $ 25.77
4) $ 44.91
5) $ 18.06

DAY 26
1) $ 23.43
2) $ 20.78
3) $ 41.01
4) $ 28.46
5) $ 18.57

DAY 27
1) $ 321.31
2) $ 341.57
3) $ 291.41
4) $ 270.96
5) $ 271.49

DAY 28
1) $ 171.22
2) $ 191.31
3) $ 171.01
4) $ 271.01
5) $ 321.14

DAY 29
1) $ 312.02
2) $ 371.91
3) $ 292.22
4) $ 441.63
5) $ 171.32

DAY 30
1) $ 191.47
2) $ 412.47
3) $ 291.12
4) $ 291.52
5) $ 171.34

DAY 31
1) >
2) =
3) <
4) <
5) <
6) >
7) <
8) <
9) <
10) >

DAY 32
1) <
2) >
3) <
4) <
5) >
6) >
7) <
8) <
9) <
10) =

DAY 33
1) <
2) <
3) >
4) <
5) >
6) =
7) >
8) >
9) >
10) <

DAY 34 DAY 35 DAY 36 DAY 37 DAY 38 DAY 39 DAY 40

	DAY 34	DAY 35	DAY 36	DAY 37	DAY 38	DAY 39	DAY 40
1)	>	>	>	>	>	>	<
2)	>	>	>	>	>	<	<
3)	>	<	>	=	=	>	<
4)	<	>	>	>	>	>	<
5)	<	<	<	<	>	<	<
6)	>	>	<	>	<	>	<
7)	<	<	>	>	>	<	<
8)	<	<	>	<	<	<	>
9)	=	<	>	=	<	<	<
10)	>	>	<	<	>	<	>

	DAY 61	DAY 62	DAY 63	DAY 64	DAY 65
1)	375 cents	51 cents	324 cents	150 cents	33 cents
2)	309 cents	77 cents	28 cents	88 cents	377 cents
3)	330 cents	12 cents	205 cents	500 cents	86 cents
4)	402 cents	625 cents	190 cents	19 cents	645 cents
5)	655 cents	257 cents	220 cents	600 cents	375 cents
6)	96 cents	108 cents	201 cents	330 cents	527 cents
7)	165 cents	63 cents	77 cents	272 cents	92 cents
8)	16 cents	650 cents	675 cents	27 cents	19 cents
9)	530 cents	228 cents	493 cents	494 cents	362 cents
10)	95 cents	60 cents	100 cents	272 cents	193 cents

	DAY 66	DAY 67	DAY 68	DAY 69	DAY 70
1)	24 cents	355 cents	305 cents	480 cents	9 cents
2)	223 cents	26 cents	260 cents	100 cents	535 cents
3)	12 cents	200 cents	98 cents	650 cents	678 cents
4)	990 cents	410 cents	205 cents	115 cents	56 cents
5)	150 cents	151 cents	245 cents	205 cents	310 cents
6)	115 cents	33 cents	425 cents	314 cents	23 cents
7)	324 cents	365 cents	465 cents	417 cents	32 cents
8)	255 cents	550 cents	335 cents	37 cents	465 cents
9)	177 cents	279 cents	85 cents	113 cents	248 cents
10)	43 cents	375 cents	254 cents	147 cents	465 cents

	DAY 71	DAY 72	DAY 73	DAY 74	DAY 75
1)	$26.25	$18.11	$18.66	$29.54	$19.36
2)	$151.94	$22.77	$28.20	$13.80	$18.51
3)	$14.62	$21.22	$224.31	$16.77	$9.64
4)	$30.94	$22.71	$17.13	$29.07	$27.37
5)	$14.13	$13.61	$147.52	$154.80	$24.32
6)	$22.19	$271.35	$21.20	$26.02	$30.46
7)	$20.20	$18.94	$34.53	$238.02	$8.51
8)	$228.40	$33.18	$20.82	$18.90	$118.13
9)	$19.94	$6.52	$5.47	$7.91	$29.42
10)	$10.37	$131.22	$27.07	$20.51	$246.92

	DAY 76	DAY 77	DAY 78	DAY 79	DAY 80
1)	$20.20	$27.40	$18.89	$25.08	$38.14
2)	$34.97	$22.23	$20.83	$25.04	$35.40
3)	$147.79	$124.12	$165.21	$126.76	$155.16
4)	$29.19	$27.08	$35.65	$29.08	$29.11
5)	$19.60	$13.92	$23.78	$14.80	$22.54
6)	$6.14	$9.38	$8.30	$12.26	$12.70
7)	$25.10	$30.23	$18.19	$22.38	$25.30
8)	$373.79	$394.03	$405.80	$385.06	$433.38
9)	$19.99	$28.25	$30.68	$18.92	$41.65
10)	$25.95	$33.89	$26.06	$18.46	$26.77

	DAY 81	DAY 82	DAY 83	DAY 84	DAY 85
1)	$15.58	$8.89	$3.30	$6.11	$13.90
2)	$0.43	$2.42	$5.18	$6.27	$13.36
3)	$6.75	$1.87	$4.83	$5.01	$13.29
4)	$3.05	$1.14	$19.92	$19.96	$2.54
5)	$0.05	$8.72	$16.89	$18.83	$1.02
6)	$5.75	$1.68	$0.96	$3.04	$9.99
7)	$4.97	$6.99	$8.13	$19.27	$1.37
8)	$10.63	$13.70	$17.52	$31.48	$15.42
9)	$19.94	$3.37	$5.07	$1.29	$18.71
10)	$3.76	$6.20	$6.90	$18.36	$1.45

	DAY 86	DAY 87	DAY 88	DAY 89	DAY 90
1)	$11.64	$5.84	$3.21	$3.61	$16.88
2)	$3.18	$8.60	$16.51	$8.43	$5.57
3)	$20.32	$17.16	$86.82	$91.26	$96.66
4)	$17.38	$0.48	$17.15	$13.38	$0.22
5)	$16.90	$18.81	$13.58	$17.83	$3.87
6)	$1.75	$4.26	$2.96	$0.66	$4.23
7)	$19.74	$6.23	$0.41	$16.85	$3.77
8)	$11.85	$38.48	$39.71	$10.67	$35.82
9)	$5.36	$1.46	$6.37	$11.03	$2.14
10)	$2.68	$6.95	$9.87	$18.12	$19.47

Made in the USA
Monee, IL
17 June 2024